Gullible's
TRAVAILS
Ed.
Brian RIX

This book contains some of Willie Rushton's last work before his unexpected death on 11th December 1996. Mencap is extremely grateful for his support and he will be sadly missed

TRAVELS

INTO SEVERAL

Remote Nations

OF THE

WORLD.

IN FOUR PARTS

By no less than twenty-three authors
and two illustrators, all of whom are
contributing their royalties to Mencap

LONDON:
Published by André Deutsch
at 106 Great Russell Street
WC1B 3LJ
MCMXCVI

Gullible's Travails

Compiled and edited by

BRIAN RIX

Illustrated by

WILLIE RUSHTON

ANDRE DEUTSCH

Proceeds from Gullible's Travails will be donated to
Mencap Trading Ltd., a wholly owned trading subsidiary
of The Royal Society for Mentally Handicapped Children
and Adults (Registered Charity No. 222377) to which it
covenants all its taxable profits.

First published in 1996 by
André Deutsch Limited
106 Great Russell Street
London WC1B 3LJ

CIP data for this title is available
from the British Library

ISBN 0 233 99010 0

Printed in Great Britain by
WBC, Bridgend

CONTENTS

PART I: A VOYAGE TO THE COUNTRIES OF THE
EUROPEAN UNION

1 Never Stop on the Motorway   13
  Jeffrey Archer

2 Way Upstream   27
  Alan Ayckbourn

3 In a Little Spanish Town   40
  Alan Coren

4 That's Amazing, Brainians!   47
  Ben Elton

5 Any Port in a Storm   51
  Clement Freud

6 Give a Dog a Bad Name   57
  Roy Hattersley

7 The Yo-Yo   64
  P. D. James

8 The Wesleyan Method   79
  Anon. (attributed to Rik Mayall)

9 Laura Norder   82
  John Mortimer

10 April in Paris?   93
  Brian Rix

PART II: A VOYAGE TO THE AMERICAS

1 Stars at Tallapoosa   101
  William Boyd

2 A Hitchhiker's Guide to the Andes   111
  Miles Kington

3 History Oozes from Every Stone in the Place   116
  Bernard Levin

4   Frozen in Time   126
    Brian Rix

5   A Night out in Llamac   130
    Matthew Parris

6   Travels in Fulham and Argentina   149
    Tim Rice

7   Goat Hurling by Moonlight   155
    Ralph Steadman

PART III: A VOYAGE TO THE SOUTHERN HEMISPHERE

1   In the Event of an Emergency a Member of the Crew
    will Drop Down in Front of You   161
    John Chapman

2   It Runs in the Family   168
    Ray Cooney

3   A Hand of Cards   174
    Michael Frayn

4   Tusitala: Robert Louis Stevenson in the South Seas 180
    Leslie Thomas

PART IV: A VOYAGE TO THE INDIAN SUBCONTINENT AND
THENCE TO THE WESTERING REACHES OF THE
IBERIAN PENINSULA

1   An Arranged Marriage   193
    Melvyn Bragg

2   Bombay Taxi   200
    Jamie Rix

3   Do You Come Here Often?   205
    Jonathan Rix

4   What's in a Name?   210
    Brian Rix

Envoi   216

A LETTER FROM BRIAN RIX
TO HIS PUBLISHER
TOM ROSENTHAL

I hope you will be ready to own publicly, whenever you shall be called to it, that by your great and frequent urgency you prevailed on me to compile a final version of my travels and those of divers authors, by mid-March in the year of Our Lord, one thousand nine hundred and ninety-six. But I do not remember I gave you power to consent that anything should be omitted. When I formerly hinted to you something of this in a letter, you were pleased to answer that you were afraid of giving offence; that the Yahoos were very watchful over the press, and apt not only to interpret but to punish everything which looked to be a poor facsimile (as I think you called it) of Jonathan Swift's inimitable style.

I do in the next place complain of my own great want of judgement, in being prevailed upon by my friends to ignore your entreaties and suffer my Travails – and those of others – to be published exactly as I had wished. In truth, the composition of the Swift masterpiece so exactly conforms to the chapter headings for this little book that I chose to treat your blandishments with disdain and must take full responsibility for so doing – as I must for dividing the book into four parts, arranging the authors according to the disposition of their surnames, indulging in the time-honoured practice of nepotism, by persuading my two sons – authors both – to add their talents to an otherwise sparse visit to the Indian subcontinent, and for the inclusion of the drawings of Mr Willie Rushton in place of the ancient, apocryphal charts which they replace.

However, given that no attempt has been made to

emulate the great writer in any other particular and expressing the pious hope that you will publish my next work, I must assure you that I have now done with all such visionary schemes for ever.

Unless this makes loadsamoney for Mencap, that is . . .

2 April 1996

THE PUBLISHER
TO THE READER

The Editor of these Travails, Lord Rix, is my ancient and intimate friend. There is, however, *no* relation between us by my mother's side, my father's side – or any other bit on the side for that matter. About twenty years ago, Lord Rix (then yet-to-be-ennobled unadorned Mr Brian Rix), growing weary of losing his trousers to entertain the public, eschewed the world of Thespis, wrote the first volume of his autobiography – *My Farce from My Elbow* – for the publishers I then represented (who shall be nameless, though their initials are S & W), and became the Secretary-General of the Royal Society for Mentally Handicapped Children & Adults – Mencap – retiring from that position in 1987 and being elevated to the position of Chairman of that august body six months later, in which office he still is held in good stead among his neighbours and his fellow Peers in the Upper House.

Before he compiled these papers, he submitted to me the unhappy story of his unfulfilled journey to Paris, suggesting that this might be the basis for a book of Travellers' Tales, contributed by the great and the good in the literary world – as well as others less well known – with the liberty to dispose of them as I should think fit. I have carefully perused them three times; the style is very plain and simple; and the only fault I can find is that the authors and illustrators may not have received the praise which is their due for such open-handed generosity – and also for composing many original works, with no reference, whatsoever, to their culinary delights or their transient and embarrassing moments, these being the usual contributions to a charitable work of this kind.

I have found no reason to be bold and strike out

innumerable passages to the winds and tides. Fortunately, no author has seen fit to insert such turgid information, other than the Editor himself, ascribing a change of wind direction to his enforced exit from Portugal, in the last chapter of this book. Otherwise the Editor has been able to fit the work as much as possible to the capacity of the readers.

For any further particulars relating to the Editor, the reader will receive satisfaction from the first part of the book, Chapter 10, and – as already stated, in the last. As for the remaining twenty-two authors and two illustrators, their credits prefix their stories. They deserve more.

PART 1

A VOYAGE TO THE COUNTRIES OF THE EUROPEAN UNION

1

NEVER STOP ON
THE MOTORWAY
Jeffrey Archer

The author (Lord Archer of Weston-Super-Mare) is almost as well known and hugely successful as an (occasional) charity auctioneer and politician as he is as a constantly best-selling writer, with breathtaking sales all over the world. Here he describes a terrifying drive by a woman who does stop on the motorway. Perhaps nervous drivers should read this story a little later, or at least lock your car doors until then. First published in Twelve Red Herrings *(HarperCollins, 1994).*

Diana had been hoping to get away by five, so she could be at the farm in time for dinner. She tried not to show her true feelings when at 4.37 her deputy, Phil Haskins, presented her with a complex twelve-page document that required the signature of a director before it could be sent out to the client. Haskins didn't hesitate to remind her that they had lost two similar contracts that week.

It was always the same on a Friday. The phones would go quiet in the middle of the afternoon and then, just as she thought she could slip away, an authorisation would land on her desk. One glance at this particular document and Diana knew there would be no chance of escaping before six.

The demands of being a single parent as well as a director of a small but thriving City company meant there were few moments left in any day to relax, so when it came to the one weekend in four that James and Caroline spent with her ex-husband, Diana would try to leave the office a little earlier than usual to avoid getting snarled up in the weekend traffic.

She read through the first page slowly and made a couple of emendations, aware that any mistake made hastily on a Friday night could be regretted in the weeks to come. She glanced at the clock on her desk as she signed the final page of the document. It was just flicking over to 5.51.

Diana gathered up her bag and walked purposefully towards the door, dropping the contract on Phil's desk without bothering to suggest that he have a good weekend. She suspected that the paperwork had been on his desk since nine o'clock that morning, but that holding it until 4.37 was his only means of revenge now that she had been made head of department. Once she was safely in the lift, she pressed the button for the basement carpark, calculating that the delay would probably add an extra hour to her journey.

She stepped out of the lift, walked over to her Audi estate, unlocked the door and threw her bag onto the back seat. When she drove up onto the street the stream of twilight traffic was just about keeping pace with the pin-striped pedestrians who, like worker ants, were hurrying towards the nearest hole in the ground.

She flicked on the six o'clock news. The chimes of Big Ben rang out, before spokesmen from each of the three main political parties gave their views on the European election results. John Major was refusing to comment on his future. The Conservative Party's explanation for its poor showing was that only thirty-six per cent of the country had bothered to go to the polls. Diana felt guilty – she was among the sixty-four per cent who had failed to register their vote.

The newscaster moved on to say that the situation in

Bosnia remained desperate, and that the UN was threatening dire consequences if Radovan Karadzik and the Serbs didn't come to an agreement with the other warring parties. Diana's mind began to drift – such a threat was hardly news any longer. She suspected that if she turned on the radio in a year's time they would probably be repeating it word for word.

As her car crawled round Russell Square, she began to think about the weekend ahead. It had been over a year since John had told her that he had met another woman and wanted a divorce. She still wondered why, after seven years of marriage, she hadn't been more shocked – or at least angry – at his betrayal. Since her appointment as a director, she had to admit they had spent less and less time together. And perhaps she had become anaesthetised by the fact that a third of the married couples in Britain were now divorced or separated. Her parents had been unable to hide their disappointment, but then they had been married for forty-two years.

The divorce had been amicable enough, as John, who earned less than she did – one of their problems, perhaps – had given in to most of her demands. She had kept the flat in Putney, the Audi estate and the children, to whom John was allowed access one weekend in four. He would have picked them up from school earlier that afternoon, and, as usual, he'd return them to the flat in Putney around seven on Sunday evening.

Diana would go to almost any lengths to avoid being left on her own in Putney when they weren't around and although she regularly grumbled about being landed with the responsibility of bringing up two children without a father, she missed them desperately the moment they were out of sight.

She hadn't taken a lover and she didn't sleep around. None of the senior staff at the office had ever gone further than asking her out to lunch. Perhaps because only three of them were unmarried – and not without reason. The one person she might have considered having a relationship with had made it abundantly clear that he only wanted to spend the night with her, not the days.

In any case, Diana had decided long ago that if she was to be taken seriously as the company's first woman director, an office affair, however casual or short-lived, could only end in tears. Men are so vain, she thought. A woman only had to make one mistake and she was immediately labelled as promiscuous. Then every other man on the premises either smirks behind your back, or treats your thigh as an extension of the arm on his chair.

Diana groaned as she came to a halt at yet another red light. In twenty minutes she hadn't covered more than a couple of miles. She opened the glove box on the passenger side and fumbled in the dark for a cassette. She found one and pressed it into the slot, hoping it would be Pavarotti, only to be greeted by the strident tones of Gloria Gaynor assuring her 'I will survive'. She smiled and thought about Daniel, as the light changed to green.

She and Daniel had read Economics at Bristol University in the early 1980s, friends but never lovers. Then Daniel met Rachael, who had come up a year after them, and from that moment he had never looked at another woman. They married the day he graduated, and after they returned from their honeymoon Daniel took over the management of his father's farm in Bedfordshire. Three children had followed in quick succession, and Diana had been proud when she was asked to be godmother to Sophie, the eldest. Daniel and Rachael had now been married for twelve years, and Diana felt confident that they wouldn't be disappointing *their* parents with any suggestion of a divorce. Although they were convinced she led an exciting and fulfilling life, Diana often envied their gentle and uncomplicated existence.

She was regularly asked to spend the weekend with them in the country, but for every two or three invitations Daniel issued, she only accepted one – not because she wouldn't have liked to join them more often, but because since her divorce she had no desire to take advantage of their hospitality.

Although she enjoyed her work, it had been a bloody week. Two contracts had fallen through, James had been dropped from the school football team, and Caroline had never stopped telling her that her father didn't mind her watching television when she ought to be doing her prep.

Another traffic light changed to red.

It took Diana nearly an hour to travel the seven miles out of the city, and when she reached the first dual carriageway, she glanced up at the A1 sign, more out of habit than to seek guidance, because she knew every yard of the road from her office to the farm. She tried to increase her speed, but it was quite impossible, as both lanes remained obstinately crowded.

'Damn.' She had forgotten to get them a present, even a decent bottle of claret. 'Damn,' she repeated: Daniel and Rachael always did the giving. She began to wonder if she could pick something up on the way, then remembered there was nothing but service stations between here and the farm. She couldn't turn up with yet another box of chocolates they'd never eat. When she reached the roundabout that led onto the A1, she managed to push the car over fifty for the first time. She began to relax, allowing her mind to drift with the music.

There was no warning. Although she immediately slammed her foot on the brakes, it was already too late. There was a dull thump from the front bumper, and a slight shudder rocked the car.

A small black creature had shot across her path, and despite her quick reactions, she hadn't been able to avoid hitting it. Diana swung onto the hard shoulder and screeched to a halt, wondering if the animal could possibly have survived. She reversed slowly back to the spot where she thought she had hit it as the traffic roared past her.

And then she saw it, lying on the grass verge – a cat that had crossed the road for the tenth time. She stepped out of the car, and walked towards the lifeless body. Suddenly Diana felt sick. She had two cats of her own, and she knew she would never be able to tell the children what she had done. She picked up the dead animal and laid it gently in the ditch by the roadside.

'I'm so sorry,' she said, feeling a little silly. She gave it one last look before walking back to her car. Ironically, she had chosen the Audi for its safety features.

She climbed back into the car and switched on the ignition to find Gloria Gaynor was still belting out her opinion of men. She turned her off, and tried to stop thinking about the cat as she waited for a gap in the traffic large enough to allow her to ease her way back into the slow lane. She eventually succeeded, but was still unable to erase the dead cat from her mind.

Diana had accelerated up to fifty again when she suddenly became aware of a pair of headlights shining through her rear windscreen. She put up her arm and waved in her rear-view mirror, but the lights continued to dazzle her. She slowed down to allow the vehicle to pass, but the driver showed no interest in doing so. Diana began to wonder if there was something wrong with her car. Was one of her lights not working? Was the exhaust billowing smoke? Was . . .

She decided to speed up and put some distance between herself and the vehicle behind, but it remained within a few yards of her bumper. She tried to snatch a look at the driver in her rear-view mirror, but it was hard to see much in the harshness of the lights. As her eyes became more accustomed to the glare, she could make out the silhouette of a large black van bearing down on her, and what looked like a young man behind the wheel. He seemed to be waving at her.

Diana slowed down again as she approached the next roundabout, giving him every chance to overtake her on the outside lane, but once again he didn't take the opportunity, and just sat on her bumper, his headlights still undimmed. She waited for a small gap in the traffic coming from her right. When one appeared she slammed her foot on the accelerator, shot across the roundabout and sped on up the A1.

She was rid of him at last. She was just beginning to relax and to think about Sophie, who always waited up so that she could read to her, when suddenly those high-beam headlights were glaring through her rear windscreen and blinding her once again. If anything, they were even closer to her than before.

She slowed down, he slowed down. She accelerated, he accelerated. She tried to think what she could do next, and began waving frantically at passing motorists as they sped by, but they remained oblivious to her predicament. She tried to think of other ways she might alert someone, and suddenly recalled that when she had joined the board of the company they had suggested she have a car phone fitted. Diana had decided it could wait until the car went in for its next service, which should have been a fortnight ago.

She brushed her hand across her forehead and removed a film of perspiration, thought for a moment, then manoeuvred her car into the fast lane. The van swung across after her, and hovered so close to her bumper that she became fearful that if she so much as touched her brakes she might unwittingly cause an enormous pile-up.

Diana took the car up to ninety, but the van wouldn't be shaken off. She pushed her foot further down on the accelerator and touched a hundred, but it still remained less than a car's length behind.

She flicked her headlights onto high-beam, turned on her hazard lights and blasted her horn at anyone who dared to remain in her path. She could only hope that the police might see her, wave her onto the hard shoulder and book her for speeding. A fine would be infinitely preferable to a crash with a young tearaway, she thought, as the Audi estate passed a hundred and ten for the first time in its life. But the black van couldn't be shaken off.

Without warning, she swerved back into the middle lane and took her foot off the accelerator, causing the van to draw level with her, which gave her a chance to look at the driver for the first time. He was wearing a black leather jacket and pointing menacingly at her. She shook her fist at him and accelerated away, but he simply swung across behind her like an Olympic runner determined not to allow his rival to break clear.

And then she remembered, and felt sick for a second time that night. 'Oh my God,' she shouted aloud in terror. In a flood, the details of the murder that had taken place on the same road a few months before came rushing back to her. A woman had been raped before having her throat cut with a knife with a serrated edge and dumped in a ditch. For weeks there had been signs posted on the A1 appealing to passing motorists to phone a certain number if they had any information that might assist the police with their enquiries. The signs had now disappeared, but the police were still searching for the killer. Diana began to tremble as she remembered their warning to all woman drivers: 'Never stop on the motorway'.

A few seconds later she saw a road sign she knew well. She had reached it far sooner than she had anticipated. In three miles she would have to leave the motorway for the sliproad that led to the farm. She began to pray that if she took her usual turning, the black-jacketed man would continue on up the A1 and she would finally be rid of him.

Diana decided that the time had come for her to speed him on his way. She swung back into the fast lane and once again put her foot down on the accelerator. She reached a hundred miles per hour for the second time as she sped past the two-mile sign. Her body was now covered in sweat, and the speedometer touched a hundred and ten. She checked her rear-view mirror, but he was still right behind her. She would have to pick the exact moment if she was to execute her plan successfully. With a mile to go, she began to look to her left, so as to be sure her timing would be perfect. She no longer needed to check in her mirror to know that he would still be there.

The next signpost showed three diagonal white lines, warning her that she ought to be on the inside lane if she intended to leave the motorway at the next junction. She kept the car in the outside lane at a hundred miles per hour until she spotted a large enough gap. Two white lines appeared by the roadside: Diana knew she would have only one chance to make her escape. As she passed the sign with a single white line on it she suddenly swung across the road at ninety miles per hour, causing cars in the middle and inside lanes to throw on their brakes and blast out their angry opinions. But Diana didn't care what they thought of her, because she was now travelling down the sliproad to safety, and the black van was speeding on up the A1.

She laughed out loud with relief. To her right, she could see the steady flow of traffic on the motorway. But then her laugh turned to a scream as she saw the black van cut sharply across the motorway in front of a lorry, mount the grass verge and career onto the sliproad, swinging from side to side. It nearly drove over the edge and into a ditch, but somehow managed to steady itself, ending up a few yards behind her, its light once again glaring through her rear windscreen.

When she reached the top of the sliproad, Diana turned left in the direction of the farm, frantically trying to work out what she should do next. The nearest town was about twelve miles away on the main road, and the farm was only seven, but five of those miles were down a winding, unlit country lane. She checked her petrol gauge. It was nearing empty, but there should still be enough in the tank for her to consider either option. There was less than a mile to go before she reached the turning, so she had only a minute in which to make up her mind.

With a hundred yards to go, she settled on the farm. Despite the unlit lane, she knew every twist and turn, and she felt confident that her pursuer wouldn't. Once she reached the farm she could be out of the car and inside the house long before he could catch her. In any case, once he saw the farmhouse, surely he would flee.

The minute was up. Diana touched the brakes and skidded into a country road illuminated only by the moon.

Diana banged the palms of her hands on the steering wheel. Had she made the wrong decision? She glanced up at her rear-view mirror. Had he given up? Of course he hadn't. The back of a Land Rover loomed up in front of her. Diana slowed down, waiting for a corner she knew well, where the road widened slightly. She held her breath, crashed into third gear, and overtook. Would a head-on collision be preferable to a cut throat? She rounded the bend and saw an empty road ahead of her. Once again she pressed her foot down, this time managing to put a clear seventy, perhaps even a hundred, yards between her and her pursuer, but this only offered her a few moments' respite. Before long the familiar headlights came bearing down on her once again.

With each bend Diana was able to gain a little time as the van continued to lurch from side to side, unfamiliar with the road, but she never managed a clear break of more than a few seconds. She checked the mileometer. From the turn-off on the main road to the farm it was just over five miles, and she must have covered about two by now. She began to watch each tenth of a mile clicking up, terrified at the thought of the van overtaking her and forcing her into the ditch. She stuck determinedly to the centre of the road.

Another mile passed, and still he clung to her. Suddenly she saw a car coming towards her. She switched her headlights to full beam and pressed on the horn. The other car retaliated by mimicking her actions, which caused her to slow down and brush against the hedgerow as they shot past each other. She checked the mileometer once again. Only two miles to go.

Diana would slow down and then speed up at each familiar bend in the road, making sure the van was never given enough room to pull level with her. She tried to concentrate on what she should do once the farmhouse came into sight. She reckoned that the drive leading up to the house must be about half a mile long. It was full of potholes and bumps which Daniel had often explained he couldn't afford to have repaired. But at least it was only wide enough for one car.

The gate to the driveway was usually left open for her, though on the odd rare occasion Daniel had forgotten, and she'd had to get out of the car and open it for herself. She couldn't risk that tonight. If the gate was closed, she would have to travel on to the next town and stop outside the Crimson Kipper, which was always crowded at this time on a Friday night, or, if she could find it, on the steps of the local police station. She checked her petrol gauge again. It was now touching red. 'Oh my God,' she said, realising she might not have enough petrol to reach the town.

She could only pray that Daniel had remembered to leave the gate open.

She swerved out of the next bend and speeded up, but once again she managed to gain only a few yards, and she knew that within seconds he would be back in place. He was. For the next few hundred yards they remained within feet of each other, and she felt certain he must run into the back of her. She didn't once dare to touch her brakes – if they crashed in that lane, far from any help, she would have no hope of getting away from him.

She checked her mileometer. A mile to go.

'The gate must be open. It must be open,' she prayed. As she swung round the next bend, she could make out the outline of the farmhouse in the distance. She almost screamed with relief when she saw the lights were on in the downstairs rooms.

She shouted, 'Thank God!' then remembered the gate again, and changed her plea to 'Dear God, let it be open.' She would know what needed to be done as soon as she came round the last bend. 'Let it be open, just this once,' she pleaded. 'I'll never ask for anything again, ever.' She swung round the final bend only inches ahead of the black van. 'Please, please, please.' And then she saw the gate.

It was open.

Her clothes were now drenched in sweat. She slowed down, wrenched the gearbox into second, and threw the car between the gap and into the bumpy driveway, hitting the gatepost on her right-hand side as she careered on up towards the house. The van didn't hesitate to follow her, and was still only inches behind as she straightened up. Diana kept her hand pressed down on the horn as the car bounced and lurched over the mounds and potholes.

Flocks of startled crows flapped out of overhanging branches, screeching as they shot into the air. Diana began screaming, 'Daniel! Daniel!' Two hundred yards ahead of her, the porch light went on.

Her headlights were now shining onto the front of the house, and her hand was still pressed on the horn. With a hundred yards to go, she spotted Daniel coming out of the front door, but she didn't slow down, and neither did the van behind her. With fifty yards to go she began flashing her lights at Daniel. She could now make out the puzzled, anxious expression on his face.

With thirty yards to go she threw on her brakes. The heavy estate car skidded across the gravel in front of the house, coming to a halt in the flowerbed just below the kitchen window. She heard the screech of brakes behind her. The leather-jacketed man, unfamiliar with the terrain, had been unable to react quickly enough, and as soon as his wheels touched the gravelled forecourt he began to skid out of control. A second later the van came crashing into the back of her car, slamming it against the wall of the house and shattering the glass in the kitchen window.

Diana leapt out of the car, screaming, 'Daniel! Get a gun, get a gun!' She pointed back at the van. 'That bastard's been chasing me for the last twenty miles!'

The man jumped out of the van and began limping towards them. Diana ran into the house. Daniel followed and grabbed a shotgun, normally reserved for rabbits, that was leaning against the wall. He ran back outside to face the unwelcome visitor, who had come to a halt by the back of Diana's Audi.

Daniel raised the shotgun to his shoulder and stared straight at him. 'Don't move or I'll shoot,' he said calmly.

And then he remembered the gun wasn't loaded. Diana ducked back out of the house, but remained several yards behind him.

'Not me! Not me!' shouted the leather-jacketed youth, as Rachael appeared in the doorway.

'What's going on?' she asked nervously.

'Ring for the police,' was all Daniel said, and his wife quickly disappeared back into the house.

Daniel advanced towards the terrified-looking young man, the gun aimed squarely at his chest.

'Not me! Not me!' he shouted again, pointing at the Audi. 'He's in the car!' He quickly turned to face Diana. 'I saw him get in when you were parked on the hard shoulder. What else could I have done? You just wouldn't pull over.'

Daniel advanced cautiously towards the rear door of the car and ordered the young man to open it slowly, while he kept the gun aimed at his chest.

The youth opened the door, and quickly took a pace backwards. The three of them stared down at a man crouched on the floor of the car. In his right hand he held a long-bladed knife with a serrated edge. Daniel swung the barrel of the gun down to point at him, but said nothing.

The sound of a police siren could just be heard in the distance.

2

WAY UPSTREAM
Alan Ayckbourn

The author, arguably the most prolific and most praised English playwright of the second half of this century, is surely worthy of greater recognition than the CBE which he received in 1987. Be that as it may, the first scene of this play paints a vividly accurate picture of the average British reaction to new holiday surroundings – whether on a hired boat, an expensive cruise, or anywhere else, for that matter. First presented at the author's own theatre in Scarborough, the Stephen Joseph Theatre in the Round, on 2 October 1981, Way Upstream *transferred to the Royal National Theatre on 4 October 1982.*

ACT I

A river. The River Orb, in fact. The first evening.

We are already considerably inland. Were it, say, the Thames we would probably be in the region of Maidenhead. During the course of the action, we will travel even further upstream some hundred miles where the Orb is far narrower and shallower and becomes finally unnavigable. The River Orb passes through the most picturesque and deserted of the English countryside. One of the last partially undiscovered rivers.

Only one craft is visible, the 'Hadforth Bounty'. A smallish

four-berth cabin cruiser of perhaps 25–30 feet in length, well-appointed, a smart unpretentious little hire craft.

It is now well after ten at night on a mild August evening with maybe just a little moonlight. For a moment, silence except for the gentle lap of the water against the boat, the splash of a water creature and the cry of a nightbird. After a second, the sound of voices approaching. Then the beams of torches as people make their way along the towpath towards us.

Leading the way is Keith Taylor, a man in his mid to late thirties but clinging a little to the belief that he appears younger. He carries one of the torches and is also laden with cases and belongings. If asked, Keith would probably describe himself as a natural leader – a role he is at present busily fulfilling. Close behind him comes his wife, June, about the same age and also laden. She is attractive and positive and is currently in a filthy temper which she is anxious to let everyone know about.

Behind her, Emma, a pleasant, rather nervous, unflamboyant sort of woman, a year or two younger than June. She, too, carries possessions and supplies including one rather large first-aid box to cater for a twelve-day holiday afloat. Finally, bringing up the rear with the second torch, comes Alistair. He is an amiable, vague, rather ineffectual man happy to play second fiddle to Keith or June and even to Emma on occasions. It becomes easy to see how pleasant a man he is to know and how infuriating to live with.

Keith . . . it must be one of these. Just a tick. (*He shines his torch on the bow of the boat*) Yes, here we are. *Hadforth Bounty*. This is the one.

Emma (*breathless*) Oh, thank goodness. It would be the last one.

Keith (*putting down his burdens*) Wait there, just wait there. (*He clambers into the cockpit*)

Emma (*while he does this*) It looks quite small, doesn't it?

Alistair (*to Keith*) Can you manage?

Keith (*struggling*) Yes, yes. I'm all right.

Emma (*gently*) Shine the torch for him, Alistair.

Alistair I am, I am.

Keith (*safely aboard*) All right, now. Would someone pass me the stuff aboard?

Alistair Oh, yes, I'll . . . (*He dithers*)

Keith June. June, my darling. Could you do something, please?

June (*beadily*) What?

Keith Could you pass me your luggage, please? I would like to get your luggage on board if I may.

June begins to do so

Thank you so much. (*As this operation continues*) I will say again. I am very sorry I have kept you all waiting. I'm sorry you had to sit in a pub for two and a half hours. I'm deeply sorry that, as a result of all that, we are starting our holiday four hours late and I am sorrier still that we are having to load this bloody boat in the pitch dark –

June nearly drops something

– careful – but it was not altogether my fault.

June (*low and fierce*) Keith. There are boats full of people back there trying to sleep.

Alistair (*unhappy at all this*) It wasn't altogether Keith's fault, you know, June.

Emma No, he couldn't help the trains.

June has now handed all her luggage on board including Keith's

Keith Thank you. May I help you aboard?

June I can manage, thank you.

Keith Right, she can manage. Fair enough.

Keith leaves June to struggle aboard whilst he goes to the doorway of the saloon and, in a moment, switches on the forward interior lights

June (*slipping as she boards*) Oh God.

Alistair (*as the lights come on*) Ah, lights.

Keith All mod cons. (*He moves to switch on the aft cabin lights*)

June (*in great difficulty, grimly*) Aaah! Damn it. Damn it. Damn it.

Emma (*gently as before*) Help her, Alistair, help her.

Alistair Oh yes. (*Starting to put his luggage down*) Do you want any help – er – June?

Keith She doesn't need help. You heard what the lady said.

June Brand new. These were brand new.

Emma (*rather impatiently*) Here, let me, June.

June I'm all right, I'm all right, I'm all right. (*She hauls herself aboard*)

Keith switches on the cockpit lights

Keith Welcome aboard, darling.

June I told you, Keith, first thing tomorrow morning I'm going straight home.

Keith Fine, fine.

June goes down the saloon steps

Thank you, Emma, I'll take those from you, shall I?

Emma starts to pass her luggage to Keith

June (*from within the saloon*) Oh, dear God. I don't believe it. I don't believe it.

Keith (*taking the large first-aid tin from Emma*) What on earth's this?

Emma First-aid box.

Keith Expecting trouble, are you?

Emma You never know.

From somewhere in the bows an incredulous cry of disgust from June

Keith I mean, I tried to phone. As soon as I saw I was going to be that late, I tried to phone. I tried to phone and say go on without me but, of course, you'd already gone. (*Offering Emma a hand aboard*) Here, Emma.

Emma Thank you.

Keith I mean, I'm not God. Am I? I can't foresee derailments.

June (*from the saloon*) They have just got to be joking. They've got to be joking.

Emma (*picking up one of the life-jackets they have brought aboard*) What are these?

Keith Life-jackets.

Emma Oh. Will we need them?

Keith Good things to have. Good things to have.

June (*emerging from the saloon*) This has simply got to be some joke. If they think anyone's going to sleep in that little broom cupboard . . .

Keith Now, come on, darling.

June Have you looked?

Keith We know you're determined to hate everything.

June No, seriously, have you looked?

Keith Yes, you've made your point, don't go on.

June No, please. Take a look. I want you to look.

Keith I don't need to look. I know what's down there. I chose the boat myself. I picked it out and I ordered it.

June You didn't order this boat. You ordered a completely different one.

Keith All right. I ordered a very similar boat.

June You ordered a bigger boat.

Keith You heard the man telling us there was engine failure.

June I heard the man putting you off with some feeble excuse . . .

Emma Come on, now, you two, it's very late. (*She starts to pick up some of the luggage in the cockpit*)

June And that is all I heard.

Keith Alistair.

Alistair (*whose thoughts have been elsewhere*) Um?

Keith Would you pass your luggage?

Alistair Oh yes, thanks.

Emma moves towards the saloon

June (*to Emma*) Just go and look in the dog kennel they laughingly call the saloon, Emma. Give yourself a laugh.

Emma Right. (*She goes into the saloon*)

June No, I mean seriously, I mean this has got to be the sickest joke I've ever heard. Four people expected to live on this for twelve days. We couldn't survive. (*She goes down into the aft cabin*)

Keith She's always the same.

Alistair (*handing him a case and smiling*) Happy holidays, eh?

Keith She is always the same.

Emma pops her head up through the forward doorway

Emma It's a sweet little kitchen.

Keith Galley.

Emma Mm?

Keith It's called a galley, love. On boats, they call it a galley.

Emma Oh. Lovely little galley, then. Sweet. (*She disappears again*)

A cry of disgust for June, below

Keith (*helping Alistair aboard*) I mean, I tried to phone. I don't honestly know what else I was supposed to have done.

Alistair Ah, well . . .

June emerges from aft

Keith Satisfactory?

June If you like sleeping on a mattress of breeze blocks, terrific.

Keith Splendid. I'm so pleased.

June And the lavatory leaves a great deal to be desired. Is that the only one?

Keith Good Lord, no. There are seven more up forward. Take your pick. What about the shower? Have you seen the shower?

June Yes. I'm dying to rush in and crouch in that. No, seriously, Keith, a joke's a joke but first thing in the morning, I'm sorry, I'm off home.

Emma comes back for more luggage, collects some and goes forward again

Keith Fine. It's your holiday. It's your choice.

June I beg your pardon, this is not my holiday. My holiday when I have one will be in a comfortable hotel, somewhere warm, with a decent bed in a room with space to swing a hamster and not in a floating rabbit hutch on an open sewer. (*She snatches up one small case and goes aft again*)

Keith (*angry*) Terrific. Isn't she terrific? Great woman to be married to. Bags of fun. That's what I've always liked about her. Fantastic sense of adventure.

Alistair OK, Keith.

Keith Of all the women there are in the world . . .

Alistair It's OK.

Keith Why do we bother, mate, why do we bother?

Emma comes up from forward again

Emma It's a lovely little front bedroom down there.

Keith Forward cabin. That's called your forward cabin.

Emma Yes. Sweet little beds.

Keith Bunks.

Emma Bunks. I think they're just brilliant the way they fit things in in the space. Terribly clever.

Keith Bless you, Emma. Thank you. That is music to my ears. Someone actually enthusing, actually showing some pleasure. So rare, thank you.

Emma Well, you have to make the best of it, don't you? (*Heading aft*) What's down here?

Keith I mean, I don't know what a man has to do, I really don't.

Alistair (*picking up a box of groceries*) I'll take these, er – this way.

Keith Forward.

Alistair Forward.

Keith What are they? Groceries?

Alistair Yes, I think they are . . .

Keith Ah, well. Stow 'em in the galley locker. We can sort things out tomorrow.

Alistair Yes.

Keith We'll try and get an early start tomorrow, shall we? First thing. When the river's at its best. Before the crowds get out.

Alistair Suits me, yes. What about . . .? (*He indicates aft*)

Keith June? Oh, she'll be all right. Means nothing. You know June.

Alistair Ah. Good. (*He goes below with the provisions*)

Keith stands alone for a moment on the deck, his hand on the wheel. He seems content

Emma re-emerges from aft

Emma It's a lovely cabin, that is. Really nice. Quite a lot of room.

Keith Yes, that's the stateroom.

Emma Oh. (*More softly*) She'll be all right, I think.

Keith Yes.

Emma The bed there's not too bad actually. Bunk. A bit lumpy.

Keith You'll be OK in the other ones, will you?

Emma Oh yes.

Keith I mean, we can probably swap round during the week. Once June's settled.

Emma No, it's very cosy in the forward, it really is.

Emma moves back to the saloon nearly colliding with Alistair coming up the steps

Alistair Sorry.

Emma Sorry.

Alistair I put the food box on the floor by the stove.

Emma Yes, I'll sort it out.

Alistair It's fairly late. Don't start too much.

Emma No, I'll just put the milk in the fridge and put the bread away and – then I'm ready for bed. Ready for bunk. (*She goes below*)

Keith She's a nice little craft this, you know, nice little craft.

Alistair Mmm. Mmm.

Keith (*leaning over the side*) Plenty of fenders, you see.

That's good, that's good. I mean, the thing about Hadforth boats is, they're not cheap but they'll never rent you rubbish. (*Checking the other side*) There, you see. The same this side.

Alistair Ah, good.

Keith This is going to be a great holiday, Alistair.

Alistair Sure.

Keith No, I mean it, really. It's going to be exciting. It's going to be a challenge. Do you realize this is the first holiday I have had personally for four years.

Alistair Really?

Keith Can you believe that? Four years. And I am going to enjoy it. With or without her.

Emma comes up

I'm saying this is going to be an exciting holiday, Emma.

Emma Oh, yes.

Keith Fresh horizons.

Emma So long as we don't sink.

Keith Sink? You'd have a job to sink this.

Alistair Which way do we go? Up or downstream?

Keith Upstream, of course.

Emma How far are we going?

Keith As far as we can. All the way.

Alistair How far's that?

Keith Armageddon Bridge. That's the limit. You can't navigate beyond that. Not in a craft this size. It's as far as we can go. Be there by next Sunday. That leaves us five days to get back. Downstream, you see. Faster. (*He clambers on to the forward deck*) Look at all this. So peaceful. Isn't this marvellous? When you think that for most of our lives we miss all this, don't we?

Alistair Yes.

Emma Yes.

They all gaze at the water for a second

Well, see you in a minute.

Alistair OK.

Emma (*to Keith*) Good-night.
Keith Good-night, Emma.

Emma goes below. There is the splash of a water-vole

Ssh.
Alistair What?
Keith Ssh. Water-vole. Hear that? Water-vole . . .
Alistair Ah.
Keith (*indicating the aft hatch*) Hatch here, you see. That's handy.
Alistair Did you have a good meeting?
Keith Oh, I think we got it. I think we've got it all right.
Alistair Well. I'm amazed.
Keith I tell you, a small firm like ours, a small factory, low overheads, competitive labour costs, we've got to win hands down. In our own line, we're out on our own. (*Examining the boat*) Beautifully built, this, you know.
Alistair Yes.
Keith Anyway, it's all Martin Cook's problem for the next twelve days. Leave it all to him.
Alistair I hope we can.
Keith Look, I've instructed Martin Cook that he is not to budge one inch from the management line and if he gets any sort of trouble from any employee, whether it be Ray Duffy or any other of his cronies, he's to throw the book at him.
Alistair Ah.
Keith It's time we got tough, Alistair. They're getting no more for nothing. Anything else, they're going to have to work for it. (*Discovering the forward hatch*) Ah, you've got a hatch this end as well. (*Opening it*) It means you can look out at the stars while you're—
Emma (*from within*) Oh, hallo.
Keith (*rapidly closing the hatch*) Oh. Sorry, my love, sorry. (*To Alistair*) Sorry. (*With an embarrassed laugh*) Didn't know they still wore those.
(*Moving back aft*) You know what'll finally bring this country down, Alistair?

Alistair What?

Keith It's when we finally give in once and for all to people like Ray Duffy. When we hand it to him on a plate. Well, I'm sorry. If he wants what's mine, he's going to have to fight me for it.

Alistair I hope it won't come to that.

Keith Don't you? You know, I think I'd rather welcome it.

June comes up from the aft, dressed for bed

June No hot water. Thought you'd like to know.

Keith (*ignoring her*) Anyway, not to worry. I am keeping a sort of eye on things, so don't worry.

June Did you hear me? I said there's no hot water.

Keith No, there won't be. We'll need to run the engines for a bit. That operates the heat exchanger.

June Well, isn't this just the jolliest little boat you could imagine? So when can we expect hot water?

Keith About ten o'clock tomorrow morning.

June Then kindly sleep well away from me tonight. (*She goes below*)

Keith Well, I'm not starting the engine now, woman, it's the middle of the night. (*To Alistair*) What does she want me to do? Does she want me to start the engine. Wake everybody up?

Alistair Do you think they're both really going to enjoy this?

Keith June's having a wonderful time. She never felt so hard done by in her life.

Alistair I meant Emma as well. She's – well, she's not really what you'd call the open-air type.

Keith She'll love it. Once we get underway. So much to see.

Alistair She's always happier in towns. I think she finds the countryside rather threatening. She doesn't even go in our garden very much and there's only about nine square feet of that. Prefers the great indoors.

Keith She can stay below then. Keep June company.

Alistair (*dubiously*) Yes. Well, if it's an early start, I'd better . . .

Keith Yes, we both should.

Alistair (*moving to the saloon*) Sleep well, then. (*He goes inside*)

Keith And you.

Alistair closes the saloon doors

(*To himself*) Great holiday. It's going to be a great holiday.

Keith gives his surroundings one more approving nod, switches off the cockpit lights and goes below into the aft cabin. He closes the doors behind him . . .

3

IN A LITTLE SPANISH TOWN
Alan Coren

The author, who modestly describes himself as a writer and broadcaster, has been the Editor of Punch *and* The Listener, *Rector of St Andrew's University, a columnist for all the main national newspapers (and currently for* The Times*), as well as the successful author of many humorous works. Here he adds to that wonderful collection with a trip to the Iberian peninsula.*

Although the threat from ETA terrorists must not be minimised, it is our experience that the British holidaymaker takes such things in his stride. And, of course, our hoteliers are going out of their way to reassure guests by every possible means. Most tourists will notice nothing out of the ordinary at all.

> Spanish Tourist Authority spokesman,
> on Radio 4's *Breakaway*

Hotel Perdicion
Las Ruinas
Costa Brava
Wednesday

Dear Auntie Doreen,

Well, here we are in viva espana as we say down here, olay, olay, and the sun coming down a treat, Kevin's head is already wrinkled like pork crackling and unable to wear free hat but never mind, it will come in useful as an oven glove, not his head, the hat, thank God he had Bakofoil round his conk is all I can say, he's a sullen bugger when he's peeling, I remember last year in, I think it was Crete, the place where they have sardine dances anyway, I remember last year when flakes kept falling off his nose into the soup, there was no living with him, all them long silences, I can see him now sitting up in bed all night, glowing like that thing on the bottom of the freezer, pilot light is it?

I thought he was going to get upset on our first day, mind, when there was this big bang and our balcony blew off, he'd hung his Aertex shirt on it to dry the armpits out on account of us having to stay four hours in the airport bus due to mines being dug out of the road in front, but it wasn't as bad as it sounds, they give us free oranges and a colouring book for the kids which Kevin said would have cost he reckoned over a pound in the shops, only trouble was little Darryl drew on the woman in front with his felt-tip and there was a bit of a row, her going on about sitting down to dinner with PIS OFF ARSNEL on her back. They come back and told us not to worry, the mines had been put in the road due to clerical error, and Kevin said typical.

Anyway, he went out on the balcony, or where the balcony would have been, and naturally said where's my bleeding leisurewear etcetera, but the manager come up and said he was terribly sorry, they were celebrating the fifty-seventh anniversary of nearly the end of the Spanish Civil War and a firework had fallen off the roof, and Kevin replied, quick as a flash, no wonder he's popular up Standard Telephone & Cables, Kevin replied first I've heard of anybody celebrating anything by blowing up somebody's shirt!

Well, the manager took his point, that is what they're paid for after all, and he was back in two minutes with a brand new floral shirt, very sheek, it's sort of a yellow, I suppose you'd call it, Kevin looks like Warren Beatty in it except for his head of course.

Lucky he was not wearing it for dinner that night, is all I can say! He had fortunately changed into an old white one you can drip dry over the bath because you know what foreign food is like with sauces and so forth, I remember one year we went to Italy or somewhere, anyway you have to go by coach, and they give us this big plate of wossname absolutely *swimming* in tomato sauce and within ten minutes Kevin had to take his No-Glu Hairpiece off, in front of everybody, because, as he went to some length to point out, they do not make them from real human hair so you have to get them dry-cleaned, and it probably cost a fortune in Italy and suppose they lost it? He got most of the meat out of it with his serviette, but it smelt of garlic all that winter, people kept moving away up the bingo.

So he was wearing his old white shirt as a precaution, and he must be physic, because one minute he was looking at his paiella and next minute it had exploded, there was bits of prawn everywhere. Naturally, he called the waiter across and said oy, I never bloody ordered this, did I, and the head waiter came over and apologised and said there'd been a mix-up in the kitchen and brought him double-egg-chips-and-beans, and Kevin said that's a bit more bloody like it. He doesn't like making a fuss, but you have to show these people who's boss, after all, it's not as if you weren't paying for it.

Darryl and Kylie and Sharon all had the fish finger special and were sick all over the lift afterwards, which was particularly embarrassing for Sharon, being fourteen and with a big bust due to being on the pill. Girls are sensitive at that age, and the manager calling the doctor only made matters worse, his hands were all over her, I don't think they have the same medical ethics in Spain, if he had done it at home he'd have been in the *Sun*, anyway he said whatever it was it was definitely not terrorist rat poison in the batter, any talk of terrorist rat poison was idle gossip, he would personally stake his reputation on the fact that none of it was down to terrorist rat poison. After he'd gone Kevin said typical, they probably want us to think it's terrorist rat poison to disguise the fact that it was their lousy cooking, he would ask for a refund at the earliest opportunity, the brochure could call it oat cuisine until it was blue in the face but oat cuisine was not something that ended up on the floor of a lift. Not much gets past Kevin!

They brought us breakfast in bed next morning, and I said that's nice, Kevin, and Kevin said hang about, we never asked for this, I bet there's a room service charge, and then the waiter pulled a gun out, and Kevin said what did I tell you, he only wants a bloody tip on top of it! But the waiter said no he didn't, he was a free Basque and we were his hostages, and Kevin said sod that, this holiday is costing £159 a head not to mention deckchairs, also six hours in Gatwick due to baggage-handlers' strike and would the waiter care to step out on the balcony and discuss it like a man, so the waiter stepped out onto where the balcony was before the firework blew it off and he fell fifteen floors into the carpark, and Kevin said next year it's Clacton, definitely.

But he cheered up on the beach. He's never been one for the beach, nothing to do he says except keep washing stuff off your feet, but there was some sort of local folk woss-name on, like the time we were in, is Morocco the one I brought you a clock back from, where the cuckoo falls out, anyway it was sort of like that, Kevin and me and every-body else had to sit behind this barbed wire they've got, and there was people with Napoleon-type hats on at one end in holes in the sand, and a lot of other people with black berets on at the other end, and they all had machine-guns. The manager came out with a tin hat on and a megaphone and said not to worry, it was all being done for a film, and Kevin said stone me, it's bloody realistic, that bloke's head's just come off, but the kids liked it, except Darryl, who had a hole shot through his Mickey Mouse bucket and his crab got out, and Kevin said bloody kids, typical, always complaining about something, a hundred-and-fifty-nine quid, but he clipped Darryl's ear and felt better.

For lunch, due to the kitchen burning down unexpected, we had to have cold meat and Kevin said sometimes this bloody country amazes me, they do everything here with bloody onions except pickle them, typical. If I was Sarson's I'd open a factory here, you could clean up. He's always been full of good commercial ideas, as you know, but his view is, what's the point of making a million, they don't let you keep it, don't talk to me about bloody governments. The way Kevin sees right through things is uncanny sometimes.

Like the business with Sharon after lunch. This little Spaniard come up while we was having what they call a siesta by the Watney's stand and he shoved this note in Kevin's hand and ran off. Kevin looked at it and informed yours truly what it said: *We have got your daughter, signed ETA.* So I said who's ETA and Kevin informed me he did not bloody know, but he was going to ask the manager, and when he come back he said the manager had told him it stood for English Tourist Aid, they often came and took girls off for a bit and gave them a good time, it was all part of the Anglo-Spanish relations etcetera and he'd tell Kevin more about it sometime when he wasn't quite so busy, he had to go now and see about repairing the telephone wires, they had all been cut due to gulls pecking through them.

So Kevin went back to sleep, and next thing we knew there was Sharon waking us up saying could she have a hundred pesetas for a Coke, she had just been given a right seeing-to by this sniper with a big Kalashnikov and it made her thirsty. And I said seeing-to? Seeing-to? What do you mean seeing-to? and Sharon said it was something they did in Spain, it was like Charlie Matthews next door, only quicker. So Kevin gave her the money, but after she'd gone he said all I seem to do is bloody shell out, if she's in pod I'll sue that bloody pill company, I'm not spending a fortune on prams etcetera at my age, if that's what this English Tourist Aid thingy calls entertainment it's a bloody disgrace, she can get all that at home, why didn't they take her on a pedalo?

4

THAT'S AMAZING, BRAINIANS!

Ben Elton

The author, who adds 'performer' to his credits, first grabbed the public's attention with his non-stop repartee as a stand-up comic. Then came his contributions to television as a writer (The Young Ones, Blackadder) and to the theatre (Gasping and Silly Cow), as well as novels (Stark, Gridlock and This Other Eden). In this offering, he leaves Planet Earth and raises an eyebrow from outer space at our travel arrangements. As someone who has battled into central London for nearly fifty years, I know just what he means . . .

High above the teaming masses of rush-hour London there recently hovered a spaceship.

This spaceship contained a group of television researchers from the Planet Brain, who were in the process of analysing humanity. They were doing this in order to compile a three-minute comedy item for their top-rated television show 'That's Amazing, Brainians!'

The researchers were pleased. Brain is populated by beings of immense intelligence and so far it had taken them only a quarter of a quarter of a single second to assimilate and comprehend humanity in its entirety.

All those things which we on Earth believe to be complex and difficult had been simplicity itself to the beings from

Brain. The situation in Beirut; what Hamlet's problem was; how to set the timer on a fourteen-day video recorder – these things were not mysteries to the Brainians: in that quarter of a quarter of a single second they had answered it all. Although in fairness it must be added that two weeks later, back on Brain, the researchers would discover that they had managed to record a documentary about Tuscany rather than *Dirty Harry*, which they really wanted to watch.

But slight slip-ups aside, the Brainians had humanity taped. They understood the rules of cricket; how the stripes get into the toothpaste; the reason there is no word in English for the back of the knee; and why people eat Fried Chicken even though they know that it will make them feel ill (because they're stupid).

But now they were stumped. They had encountered one aspect of human activity which astonished and mystified even these hardened researchers, who thought they had mastered every illogicality and lunacy that Earth had to offer. They had seen pointless war and pointless destruction; they had visited the Tate gallery; they had listened to modern jazz; they had read the novels of James Joyce; they had seen ice creams which claim to be shaped like faces but are actually shaped like amoeba – and they had understood it all. But one thing stumped them, they simply could not get their thought podules around it.

The problem was one of transport.

The Brainians could see the long thin arteries along which the humans travelled. They noted that after sunrise the humans all travelled one way and at sunset they all travelled the other way. They could see that progress was slow and congested along these arteries, that there were endless blockages, queues, bottlenecks and delays causing untold frustration and inefficiency. All this they could see quite clearly.

What was not clear to them was why. If, as was obvious, space was so restricted, why was it that each single member of this strange life form insisted on occupying perhaps fifty times its own ground surface area for the entire time it was in motion? Or not in motion, as was normally the case. The super-intelligent beings transmitted their data back to the producer of their programme and they received a right earful in reply (which was rather a lot because although Brainians are only eight inches tall, their ears are the size of wheel-barrows and have to be rolled up like blinds).

'You're mad,' bellowed the TV producer, using his inter-galactic portable phone because, like TV producers the universe over, he was having lunch. 'You're trying to tell me that they're all going in the *same* direction, travelling to much the *same* destinations and yet they're all *deliberately* impeding the progress of each other by covering six square metres of space with a large, almost completely empty tin box?'

'That's exactly what we're trying to tell you, boss, they're all stuck down there, beeping and screaming at each other.'

'Oh, go on then, let's have another bottle of wine,' said the TV producer, which naturally rather confused the researchers, but in fact the TV producer hadn't been speaking to them – his last remark was addressed at his lunch companion. Having another bottle of wine is something else which TV producers do the universe over, except in Los Angeles where people who ten years ago took cocaine in their coffee now give you the phone number of Alcoholics Anonymous if you ask for a beer.

Returning to his telephone conversation, the producer could scarcely contain his excitement.

'You're telling me,' he said, 'that a society sufficiently sophisticated to produce the internal combustion engine has not had the sophistication to develop cheap and efficient public transport?'

'Yes, boss,' said the researchers, 'it's true. There are hardly any buses, the trains are hopelessly underfunded, and hence the entire population is stuck in traffic.'

'Well, that's amazing,' said the TV producer.

'Yes, boss, it is amazing,' the researchers agreed.

'Get your asses back to Brain, we got a show.'

5

ANY PORT IN
A STORM
Clement Freud

The author (actually, Sir Clement Freud) bills himself as a writer, broadcaster and caterer. Only later in his cv do you realise (if you didn't know it already) that he was a Liberal MP from 1973 to 1987, and Rector of the University of Dundee from 1976 to 1980, as well as being a sports writer, a columnist, a cookery editor and the President of the Down's Children Association. All his multifarious talents are apparent in this tale of what might be loosely termed alcoholic abuse.

When I was 23 years old I went to the south of France to continue my catering apprenticeship at an hotel in Cannes and the Managing Director, who was very busy and spoke French very quickly, asked to see me, shook my hand, bade me sit down, told me he hoped that I would be content, and that as a gesture to international co-operation between our countries I should drink a litre of wine per week with my meals, with his compliments, and good luck. He got up. I got up. I did not see him again for a month.

As I explained, he spoke quickly; I missed the 'per week' bit, had not at that time gone metric and was surprised, when I ordered a litre of wine with my first lunch, at the size of the bottle.

My colleagues looked on admiringly as I did my best for the old *entente* and finished it within the half-hour lunch break. That night I had another litre, and the next lunch and the next evening.

In those first weeks in Cannes I became the Captain of the hotel football team, though I played rugby; bought a second-hand motorbike with sidecar which I had no licence to drive; proposed marriage to several customers and the housekeeper who was 58; and on my twenty-fourth birthday won a substantial sum of money playing No. 24 in the casino. Throughout that time I moved in the oysterlight of an alcoholic haze, mistook customers for each other, gave people the wrong room keys, the wrong messages, the wrong bills, and quite often fell asleep behind the reception desk – but I never let down the generous Managing Director. That litre of wine was drunk twice a day, and on my day off I had lunch or dinner out and then returned to the hotel to claim my tipple.

At the end of the month I saw the Managing Director for the second time. He said, and he now spoke more slowly (or I understood him better), that the reports he had received about me were less than totally satisfactory.

'It appears,' he said, 'that you drink.'

'Only,' I answered, 'what you so kindly asked me to drink for the sake of national amity.' Indeed, I assured him, there was little opportunity after that to consume other liquor, and I promised him that I had not done so.

'But you drink two litres a day,' he said, looking at his notes.

'With your compliments,' I said, belching gently and trying to get him into focus.

'I offered you one litre a week.'

There was not a lot I could say. My casino winnings went to pay my wine bills and Cannes look on an entirely new appearance – not just because it was spring. Customers emerged from their cocoons of anonymity; keys achieved an identity. The Croisette outside remained static when it had previously refused to settle down, and my eyes returned to the colour specified on page two of my passport signed by Ernest Bevin.

I have been interested in hangovers ever since.

I had, in my drinking days in France, a friend who tried hard to make me join the better-class gatherings of the Riviera. He painted, I cooked: we were both very poor. Like me, he drank red wine and dreamt of golden-coloured whisky, even whiskey (the letter 'e' between k and y denotes that it comes from some other land than Scot).

At that time, 1948, opportunities to drink hard liquor were few and far between. One day, after an especially long pause, I received a message about a party in the square at Antibes. An English yacht-owner was celebrating the remarriage of his ex-wife, and had taken over the Café des Anglais, and my friend, who knew the tycoon, had got me an invitation to attend. 'Come and call for me at my studio and we'll prepare for the evening,' he wrote. 'Be there at 5 p.m.'

I arrived punctually. He welcomed me with conspiratorial glee, and told me it was going to be just like going to the Savoy without the bill. I followed him to his kitchen, he ceremoniously got two large port glasses and a bottle of olive oil, and said, 'This lines the stomach; it is not going to be very nice but by God, we'll drink the rest of them under the table. Gulp this down and we shall be the only three-bottle men in the Alpes Maritimes.'

The party was due to start at 6 o'clock and so as not to appear over-eager we determined to delay our arrival until 6.05; the square at Antibes was fifteen minutes' fast walk. As there was nothing in the house to take away the taste of the oil before we fell on the whisky, we played a little backgammon and at 5.49 p.m. emptied our glasses, gave each other the amazed looks that pass between olive oil drinkers and trotted out into the evening.

It all went according to plan. We reached Le Café des Anglais at 6.05 and flashed our invitation card. 'Alors,' said the Propriétaire, 'that party was last night.'

My friend pawned his watch and we went to Le Café Marseillaise, where the whisky was cheaper.

The writer of a sixteenth-century recipe for 'Sallet Oyle' – to be taken with new milk – adds gloomily, 'But howe sicke you will be with the preuntion I will not heere determine.'

Goodness, I know what he meant.

When I was first commissioned in the army, I was stationed in Lancashire under a commanding officer who felt a deep sense of injury about being too old for action. He had as much interest in us, his subalterns, as I had in research into distemper. But fortunately he had a wife in whom the milk of human kindness flowed with abundance. As a result of her concern we were invited to have dinner, eight at a time; had the old man had his way we would have been given cakes and ale in the drill hall, but he did not get his way. And so it was that one autumn evening, in the company of Second Lieutenants Fisher, Flint, Fosdyke, Freemantle, Freshwater, Fretwell and Fuller, I walked down the Lancaster Road to the commanding officer's residence.

I don't remember too much about the meal other than that the Colonel's wife had asked the matron and a couple of elderly (anyone over 26 was elderly to us) nurses from the local infirmary, and while they did their best to make us feel at ease, we did our damnedest to get the staff to refill our glasses and drink the old boy into penury.

When the meal was over the ladies withdrew, the coffee arrived, as did the port, and in the silence that ensued, one of my colleagues, Fretwell – who was slightly worldlier than the rest of us – said, 'Very fine port, this sir. You know, they have excellent port at the Cat and Cucumber in Garstang.' The Colonel looked at Fretwell for a long moment before he exploded – and in justification let me remind gentle readers who are too young or possibly too old that this was a time when the average pub was lucky to have beer, let alone port-type wine, and the Cat and Cucumber in Garstang was some way below being average.

We listened while the old boy started off on the inadvisability of putting pearls before swine. 'Bloody little social upstarts,' he went on. 'Always knew it was a mistake to have these bloody dinners. Now I know I was right. Mullery, take away the decanter. Gentlemen, you may piss off back to the barracks ... and you, sir, will doubtless be going off to Garstang.' We kicked Fretwell all the way back to the barracks – a man but for whom we would certainly have ended the night less sober than we were.

About fifteen years later I was at Lord's watching a mid-week county match and, while less than compulsive events occurred on the field of play, I went to the Long Room for a drink. There I found only one other occupant, the Colonel, older but still as angry and tetchy and intimidating as I remembered. He had been a County cricketer, I was then a cricket writer for the *Observer*, and it seemed churlish not to make a gesture at conversation. The MCC is a Club, and that is what membership is all about, so I introduced myself. He nodded absently.

'I served under you in the Mixed Irish Brigade at Lancaster,' I said.

'Mmm?'

'You may recall, sir, that I had dinner with you when one of my colleagues compared your Croft's '24 to the hogwash they served at the Cat and Cucumber in Garstang.'

The old boy suddenly came to life like a clockwork toy when you release the key. An arm swung. His mouth opened and closed. He blinked. His legs carried him a step away and then a step back. I watched with admiration. He finally regained his equanimity and said:

'Let me tell you something I've been wanting to tell someone for a very long time. After you had gone overseas I found that my batman had been selling my Cockburn's '29 to the local pub, and your chap was right.'

6

GIVE A DOG
A BAD NAME
Roy Hattersley

The author, the Rt. Hon. Roy Sydney George Hattersley, PC, BSc, MP to accord him his full nomenclature and titles, could by now be the Deputy Prime Minister if the 1992 Election had been consistent with Labour's desires. Unfortunately for him, perhaps, that was not to be; but, fortunately for us, this gives him more time to be a novelist, a columnist and a broadcaster. He has kept his air of optimistic cynicism throughout, which – as a follower of Yorkshire County Cricket Club – has served him in good stead. In this story, the husband's journeys from home are of short duration – but of an extremely suspicious nature.

Cynthia was not suspicious by nature. Nor had she any reason to be. For she and John had enjoyed twenty years of unmitigated devotion. He had pandered to her silly little foibles and she admired him with a fervour which was dangerously close to idolatry. But Cynthia was a worrier. And, ever since her husband's family firm had been taken over by a German company, she had assumed that one evening he would arrive home with a large cheque and nothing to do with the rest of his life.

So when, one Wednesday morning, he set off for work an hour earlier than usual, Cynthia took it for granted that the moment of truth had come. She worried all day. But

when John got home – punctually at seven o'clock as always – she waited for him to break the bad news in his own good time. John knew best about these things. He would choose the right moment. But although he was unusually talkative over supper, there was no mention of what, by then, Cynthia had taken for granted was his impending unemployment. She thought that he was sparing her feelings for as long as possible.

John left home early on both Thursday and Friday mornings. As he left the house she asked him, trying to sound casual, if he realised that it was only half past seven. He replied that he did and went smiling on his way. Over lunch on Saturday, she emboldened herself to enquire, 'Is everything all right?' He assured her that her cooking was, as always, excellent and invited her to agree that 'Any Questions' had deteriorated during the last couple of years. It was obvious that he was keeping something from her. That night Cynthia hardly slept at all. John smiled and snored for his usual eight full hours.

On Saturday afternoon – during the walk that they had taken across Blackheath on every weekend of their marriage – she decided that she had to ask him 'right out'. It was an act of considerable courage. For she was already disconcerted by the kites which flew dangerously overhead, the bicycles which raced dangerously along the pathways and the dogs which bounded dangerously across the grass. But she forced herself. She could think of only one way to ask the question.

'Is everything all right? Things in general, I mean.'

'Of course. Why do you ask?'

'At work, I meant. No trouble there? The early mornings . . .'

'Never better.'

When he repeated, 'Why do you ask?' she replied, 'No reason, really.'

John had never and would never lie to her. But then John was not usually so dismissive! Cynthia tried to enjoy Sunday evening. And she felt serene with relief when, on

Monday morning, John was still in the bathroom at eight o'clock. She waved goodbye from the window. But as always, John was reading his paper almost before his driver had shut the car door.

Cynthia was back at the window again at half past eight that evening. For John had not returned home. At nine, fearful that he was dead on the road, she telephoned the office. The switchboard was closed, but a security guard answered. 'Can you take a message up to my husband's office?' she asked, not wanting to sound too concerned in case he was still alive.

'He's been gone two hours,' the guard told her. 'I saw him leave whilst I was clocking on. I noticed because his car was in the yard, round the back.'

John, Cynthia decided, was dying of some incurable disease and was spending the missing hours receiving some pain-relieving treatment. He was postponing the terrible moment when he had to warn her of impending widow-hood. It was exactly the sort of self-sacrifice which she should have expected. Thank heavens, she thought, that she had never even begun to doubt his fidelity. She had no idea how she should react to the awful discovery. She wanted to tell him that she knew, hold him in her arms and comfort his last days. But perhaps she had a duty to respect his heroic privacy. She telephoned her sister Kate for advice.

Kate was suspicious by nature.

'You are an ass,' she told her sister. 'It sounds like a woman to me. Is everything all right between you?'

'Yes,' said Cynthia, confident about something for the first time in days.

'In bed?' asked Kate.

'Yes.' It was not the sort of subject that Cynthia liked to talk about.

'Well, watch out for signs. Hairs on his jacket. Embarrassed moments when he pulls incriminating evidence out of his pocket. Look at his tie. If it's tied differently at night from the way it was when he left in the morning, you're in trouble.'

Cynthia told her sister that she was not prepared to listen to such disloyal rubbish. But a tiny seed of doubt had been planted. When John eventually got home that night she was so busy staring at his tie that she barely heard his apology. '. . . I didn't telephone because I kept thinking that I would get away any minute.'

The explanation was so unconvincing that even Cynthia began to fear that what her sister had predicted must be true. After all these years. John of all people. Please God, it would pass. Should she make a fuss or should she wait? Being the woman she was, she decided that waiting was best.

She did, however, almost burst into tears when, on Saturday morning, he announced that he was going to see Charlton play Derby County at The Dell that afternoon. John had not been to a football match for years. Then on Sunday morning – when, as always, he brought her breakfast in bed – he told her, 'I've got to nip into the office for a couple of hours.' He was gone before she could decide what to do. As she cooked the lunch, she made up her mind. There would have to be a confrontation, when he got home.

It was the three long black hairs that made her lose her nerve. They stood out – brazen and undeniable – on the shoulder of his tweed jacket. Such hairs, Cynthia decided, must have been on his shoulder every day for the last fortnight. But they were invisible against the background of his dark business suit. The hairs made it impossible for her to challenge him. Before they had appeared and ruined her life, it had been just possible for her to accuse him because there had been hope of a convincing denial. Now the facts were conclusive. Next day, after John had left early for work, Cynthia telephoned Kate and told her that the evidence left no room for doubt. 'The bastard,' Kate said. It did not help Cynthia to decide what to do.

That night, when John got home, he was not wearing the shoes in which he had left the house in the morning. He saw that she had noticed. 'I got drenched this morning,' he told her. 'Lucky I had this old pair of shoes in the car.'

Cynthia told herself that John never lied. But she could not help remembering that, although it had rained all day, her husband had been exposed to the elements for the time that it took him to run – twice or three times – from his door to the car and back again. It was, Cynthia decided, impossible to hide her feelings any longer. But to give herself the courage to make the awful accusation she would have to catch him in the act – well, as near to the act as dignity and decency allowed. Naturally enough, her nerve failed again.

So Cynthia suffered another week of early mornings, late nights, and furtive examination of her husband's clothes. Once, when she found what seemed to be digestive biscuit crumbs in a top-coat pocket, she almost began to hope that there was nothing more to worry about than a gastric ulcer. But John – who was notoriously sensible about his health – was eating and drinking more than usual. And he was so obviously happy.

Then, on Saturday morning when he had just 'nipped into the office to sign a couple of letters', she saw his car parked on the edge of the Heath. John was a hundred yards along the road putting money in a parking meter. But, even through her tears, Cynthia could see a shape – a long-haired shape – in the passenger seat.

Cynthia stumbled towards her husband, almost dropping her shopping basket as she ran. And as she ran she thought of what to say. All over. Please come back to me. Never again. I forgive you. It doesn't matter, we can start again. Thrown away, for what? A denial of twenty years. The past can't be forgotten. As always, it was John who spoke first.

'I'm glad.' It was, Cynthia thought, the classic response. 'I couldn't have gone on with the pretence much longer. Anyway, it's not fair to her.'

'Fair to her ...' said Cynthia bitterly, provoked into the courage to speak.

'Where she's living now is ghastly. The people are kind enough and it's comfortable. But she needs love.'

'I need love,' said Cynthia, knowing how pathetic she sounded.

'You've got to try and face it,' said John, taking his wife's arm and hurrying her towards the car.

'Face it. How can I face it?'

'You'll like her when you get to know her. She's no trouble. She'll fit in.'

'Fit in!' Cynthia could not believe what she was hearing.

'I know you won't like it. But do it for me.'

They were at the car as John half opened the door. On the passenger seat there sat a black, long-haired retriever bitch.

7

THE YO-YO
P. D. James

The author (Baroness James of Holland Park, OBE) began her professional life as a Civil Servant. Her experience as a senior official at the Home Office in the Police Department, and then the Criminal Policy Department, must have given her an acute insight into the criminal mind; a spell inside Broadcasting House as a Governor of the BBC and at the Arts Council as Chairman of the Literature Panel could possibly have been of some practical assistance as well. The Noble Lady is now one of our best and most successful mystery writers – in the world of books, television and films – as her specially written short story, 'The Yo-Yo', clearly demonstrates. Just to clear up any further mysteries, and in case any putative producers are interested, 'The Yo-Yo' remains the copyright of P. D. James and is here reproduced by kind permission of the author, care of her agents, Greene & Heaton.

I found the yo-yo the day before Christmas Eve, in the way one does come across these long-forgotten relics of the past, while I was tidying up some of the unexamined papers which clutter my elderly life. It was my seventy-third birthday and I suppose I was overtaken by a fit of *memento mori*. Most of my affairs were tidied up years ago, but there is always a muddle somewhere. Mine was in

six old box files on a top shelf of the wardrobe in my little-used spare bedroom, normally out of sight and out of mind. But now, for no particular reason, they intruded into my mind with an irritating persistence. Their contents ought to be sorted through and the papers either filed or destroyed. Henry and Margaret, my son and daughter-in-law, would expect to find that I, the most meticulous of fathers, had spared them even this minor inconvenience on my death. There was nothing else I needed to do. I was waiting, suitcase packed, for Margaret to come in the car to collect me for a family Christmas I would infinitely have preferred to spend alone in my Temple flat. To collect me. That is what we can so easily be made to feel at seventy-three; an object, not exactly precious but likely to be brittle, to be carefully collected, conscientiously cared for and as conscientiously returned. I was ready too early, as I always am. There were nearly two hours to be got through before the car arrived. Time to sort out the boxes.

The box files, bulging and one with the lid wrenched loose, were tied with thin cord. Undoing this and opening the first box, I was met by a half-forgotten nostalgic smell of old papers. I carried the box to the bed, settled down and began leafing through a miscellany of papers from my prep school days, old school reports – some of the inked comments yellowing, others as clear as if written yesterday – letters from my parents still in their fragile envelopes, with the foreign stamps torn away to give to school-friend collectors, one or two school exercise books with highly marked essays which I had probably kept to show my parents on their next furlough. Lifting one of these I discovered the yo-yo. It was just as I remembered it, bright red, glossy, tactile and desirable. The string was neatly wound with only the looped end for the finger showing. My hand closed round the smooth wood. The yo-yo precisely fitted my palm. It felt cold to the touch, even to my hand which is now seldom warm. And with that touch the memories came flooding back. The verb is trite but accurate; they came like a full tide, sweeping me back to the same day sixty years ago, 23 December 1936, the day of the murder.

I was at prep school in Surrey and was, as usual, to spend Christmas with my widowed grandmother in her small manor house in west Dorset. The rail journey was tedious, requiring two changes, and there was no local station, so she usually sent her own car and driver to collect me. But this year was different. The headmaster called me into his study to explain.

'I've had this morning a telephone call from your grandmother, Charlcourt. It appears that her chauffeur is suffering from influenza and will be unable to fetch you. I've arranged for Saunders to drive you down to Dorset in my personal car. I need Saunders until after lunch, so it will be a later arrival than usual. Lady Charlcourt has kindly offered him a bed for the night. And Mr Michaelmass will be travelling with you. Lady Charlcourt has invited him to spend Christmas at the manor, but no doubt she has already written to you about that.'

She hadn't, but I didn't say so. My grandmother wasn't fond of children and tolerated me more from family feeling – I was, after all, like her only son, the necessary heir – than from any affection. She did her dutiful best each Christmas to see that I was kept reasonably happy and out of mischief. There was a sufficiency of toys appropriate to my sex and age, purchased by her chauffeur on written suggestions from my mother, but there was no laughter, no young companionship, no Christmas decorations and no emotional warmth. I suspected that she would much have preferred to spend Christmas alone than with a bored, restless and discontented child. I don't blame her. I have reached her age and I feel exactly the same.

But as I closed the door of the headmaster's study my heart was heavy with resentment and disgust. Didn't she know anything about me or the school? Didn't she realise that the holiday would be boring enough without the sharp eyes and sarcastic tongue of Mike the Menace? He was easily the most unpopular master in the school, pedantic, over-strict, and given to that biting sarcasm which boys find more difficult to bear than shouted insults. I know now that he was a brilliant teacher. It was to Mike the Menace that I largely owe my public school scholarship. Perhaps it was this knowledge and the fact that he had been at Balliol with my father which had prompted my grandmother's invitation. My father might even have written to suggest it. I was less surprised that Mr Michaelmass had accepted. The comfort and excellent food at the manor would be a welcome change from the spartan living and institutional cooking at school.

The journey was as boring as I had expected. Instead of the elderly Hastings at the wheel, who would have let me sit in the front seat beside him and kept me happy with chat about my father's childhood, I was closeted in the back with a silent Mr Michaelmass. The glass partition between us and the driver was closed and all I could see was the back of the rigid uniform hat, which the headmaster always insisted that Saunders should wear when acting as chauffeur, and his gloved hands on the wheel.

Saunders wasn't really a chauffeur but was required to drive the headmaster when his prestige demanded this addition to his status. For the rest of the time Saunders was part groundsman, part odd-job man. His wife, frail and gentle-faced and looking as young as a girl, was matron at one of the three boarding houses. His son Timmy was a pupil at the school. Only later did I fully understand this curious arrangement. Saunders was what I had overheard one of the parents describe as 'a most superior type of man'. I never knew what personal misfortune had brought him to his job at the school. The headmaster got Saunders' and his wife's services cheaply by offering them accommodation and free education for their son. He probably paid them a pittance. If Saunders resented this, we, the boys, never knew. We got used to seeing him about the grounds, tall, white-faced, dark-haired, and, when not busy, playing always with the red yo-yo. It was a fashionable toy in the 1930s and Saunders was adept at the spectacular throws which the rest of us practised with our own yo-yos but never achieved.

Timmy was an undersized, delicate, nervous child. He sat always at the back of the class, neglected and ignored. One of the boys, a more egregious snob than the rest of us, said: 'I don't see why we have to have that creep Timmy in class with us. That's not why my father pays the fees.' But the rest of us didn't mind one way or the other, and in Mike the Menace's class Timmy was a positive asset, diverting from the rest of us the terror of that sharp, sarcastic tongue. I don't think in Mr Michaelmass's case the cruelty had anything to do with snobbery, or even that he recognised his behaviour as cruel. He was simply unable to tolerate wasting his teaching skills on an unresponsive and unintelligent boy.

But none of this occupied my mind on the journey. Sitting well apart from Mr Michaelmass in the corner of the car, I was sunk in a reverie of resentment and despair. My companion preferred to be driven in darkness as well as silence, and we had no light. But I had brought with me a paperback and a slender torch and asked him if it would disturb him if I read. He replied, 'Read by all means, boy', and sank back into the collar of his heavy tweed coat.

I took out my copy of *Treasure Island* and tried to concentrate on the small moving pool of light. Hours passed. We were driven through small towns and villages and it was a relief from boredom to look out at brightly lit streets, the decorated gaudy windows of the shops and the busy stream of late shoppers. In one village a little group of carol singers accompanied by a brass band were jangling their collecting boxes. The sound seemed to follow us as we left the brightness behind. I was, of course, familiar with the route, but Hastings normally called for me in the morning of December 23rd so that we did most of the drive in daylight. Now, sitting beside that silent figure in the gloom of the car and with blackness pressing against the windows like a heavy blanket, the journey seemed interminable. Then I sensed that we were climbing, and

soon I could hear the distant rhythmic thudding of the
sea. We must be on the coast road. It would not be long
now. I shone my torch on the face of my wrist-watch.
Half-past five. We should be at the manor in less than an
hour.

And then Saunders slowed the car and bumped gently
on to the grass verge. The car stopped. He pulled back the
glass partition and said: 'I'm sorry, sir. I need to get out. A
call of nature.'

The euphemism made me want to giggle. Mr Michaelmass hesitated for a moment, then said: 'In that case we'd
better all get out.'

Saunders came round and punctiliously opened the door.
We stepped out on to lumpy grass, and into black darkness
and the swirl of snow. The sea was no longer a background
murmur but a crashing tumult of sound. I was at first
aware of nothing but the snowflakes resting and drying on
my cheeks, the two dark figures close to me, the utter
blackness of the night and the keen salty tang of the sea.
Then, as my eyes became accustomed to the darkness, I
could see the shape of a huge rock to my left.

Mr Michaelmass said: 'Go behind that boulder, boy.
Don't take long. And don't go wandering off.'

I stepped closer to the boulder, but not behind it, and the
two figures moved out of sight, Mr Michaelmass walking
straight ahead and Saunders to the right. A minute later,
turning from the rock-face, I could see nothing, not the car
or either of my companions. It would be wise to wait until
one of them reappeared. I plunged my hand into my pocket
and, almost without thinking, took out the torch and shone
it over the headland. The beam of light was narrow but
bright. And in that moment, instantaneously, I saw the act
of murder.

Mr Michaelmass was standing very still about thirty
yards away, a dark shape outlined against the lighter sky.
Saunders must have moved up silently behind him on the
thin carpet of snow. Now, in that second when the dark
figures were caught in the beam, I saw Saunders violently

lunge forward, arms outstretched, and seemed to feel in the small of my own back the strength of that fatal push. Without a sound Mr Michaelmass disappeared from view. There had been two shadowy figures; now there was one.

Saunders knew that I had seen, how could he help it? The beam of light had been too late to stop the action, but now he turned and it shone full on his face. We were alone together on the headland. Curiously I felt absolutely no fear. I suppose that what I did feel was surprise. We moved towards each other almost like automata. I said, hearing the note of simple wonder in my voice: 'You pushed him over. You murdered him.'

He said: 'I did it for the boy. God help me, I did it for Timmy. It was him or the boy.'

I stood for a moment silently regarding him, aware again of the soft liquid touch of the snow melting on my cheeks. I shone the torch down and saw that the two sets of footprints were already no more than faint smudges on the snow. Soon they would be obliterated under that white blanket. Then, still without speaking, I turned and we walked back to the car together, almost companionably, as if nothing had happened, as if that third person was walking by our side. I have a memory, but perhaps I may be wrong, that at one place Saunders seemed to stumble and I held his arm to steady him. When we reached the car he said, his voice dull and without hope, 'What are you going to do?'

'Nothing. What is there to do. He slipped and fell over the cliff. We weren't there. We didn't see, either of us. You were with me at the time. We were both together by that rock. You never left my side.'

He said nothing for the moment, and when he did speak I had to strain my ears to hear.

'I planned it, God help me. I planned it, but it was fate. If it was meant to be, then it would be.'

The words meant little at the time but later, when I was older, I think I understood what he was saying. It was one way, perhaps the necessary way, to absolve himself from responsibility. That push hadn't been the overwhelming impulse of the moment. He had planned the deed, had chosen the place and the time. He knew exactly what he meant to do. But so much had been outside his control. He couldn't be sure that Mr Michaelmass would want to leave the car, or that he would stand so conveniently close to the edge of the cliff. He couldn't be sure that the darkness would be so absolute or that I would stand sufficiently apart. And one thing had worked against him; he hadn't known about my torch. If the attempt had failed, would he have tried again? Who can know? It was one of the many questions I never asked him.

He opened the rear door for me, suddenly standing upright, a deferential chauffeur doing his job. As I got in I turned and said, 'We must stop at the first police station and let them know what has happened. Leave the talking to me. And we'd better say that it was Mr Michaelmass, not you, who wanted to stop the car.'

I look back now with some disgust at my childish arrogance. The words had the force of a command. If he resented it he made no sign. And he did leave the talking to me, merely quietly confirming my story. I told it first at the police station in the small Dorset town which we reached within fifteen minutes. Memory is always disjointed, episodic. Some impulse of the mind presses the button and, like a colour transparency, the picture is suddenly thrown on the screen, vivid, immobile, a glowing instant fixed in time between the long stretches of dark emptiness. At the police station I remember a tall lamp with the snowflakes swirling out of darkness to die like moths against the glass, a huge coal fire in a small office which smelt of furniture polish and coffee, a sergeant, huge, imperturbable, taking down the details, the heavy oilskin capes of the policemen as they stamped out to begin the search. I had decided precisely what I would say.

'Mr Michaelmass told Saunders to stop the car and we got out. He said it was a call of nature. Saunders and I went to the left by a large boulder and Mr Michaelmass walked

72

ahead. It was so dark we didn't see him after that. We both waited for him, I suppose for about five minutes, but he still didn't appear. Then I took out my torch and we explored. We could just see his footsteps to the edge of the cliff but they were getting very faint. We still hung around and called, but he didn't reappear, so we knew what must have happened.'

The sergeant said: 'Hear anything, did you?'

I was tempted to say, 'Well I did think I heard one sharp cry, but I thought it could be a bird', but I resisted the temptation. Would there be a seagull flying in that darkness? Better to keep the story simple and stick to it. I have sent a number of men down for life because they have neglected that simple rule.

The sergeant said that he would organise a search, but that there was little chance of finding any trace of Mr Michaelmass that night. They would have to wait for first light. He added, 'And if he went over where I think he did, we may not retrieve the body for weeks.' He took the addresses of my grandmother and the school and let us go.

I have no clear memory of our arrival at the manor, perhaps because recollection is overshadowed by what happened next morning. Saunders, of course, breakfasted with the servants while I was in the dining-room with my grandmother. We were still in the middle of our toast and marmalade when the parlour maid announced that the Chief Constable, Colonel Neville, had called. My grandmother asked that he be shown into the library, and left the dining-room immediately. Less than a quarter of an hour later I was summoned.

And now my memory is sharp and clear, every word remembered as if it were yesterday. My grandmother was sitting in a high-backed leather chair before the fire. It had only recently been lit and the room struck me as chill. The wood was still crackling and the coals hadn't yet caught fire. There was a large desk set in the middle of the room where my grandfather used to work, and the Chief

Constable was sitting behind it. In front of it stood Saunders, rigid as a soldier called before his commanding officer. And on the desk, precisely placed in front of the Colonel, was the red yo-yo.

Saunders turned briefly as I entered and gave me one single look. Our eyes held for no more than three seconds before he turned away but I saw in his eyes – how could I not? – that wild mixture of fear and pleading.

I have seen it many times since from prisoners in the dock awaiting the pronouncement of my sentence, and I have never been able to encounter it with equanimity. Saunders needn't have worried; I had relished too much the power of that first decision, the heady satisfaction of being in control, to think of betraying him now or ever. And how could I betray him? Wasn't I now his accomplice in guilt?

Colonel Neville was stern-faced. He said: 'I want you to listen to my questions very carefully and tell me the exact truth.'

My grandmother said: 'Charlcourts don't lie.'

'I know that, I know that.' He kept his eyes on me. 'Do you recognise this yo-yo?'

'I think so, sir, if it's the same one.'

My grandmother broke in. 'It was found on the edge of the cliff where Mr Michaelmass fell. Saunders says that it isn't his. Is it yours?'

She shouldn't have spoken, of course. And I wondered at the time why the Chief Constable should have allowed her to be present at the interview. Later I realised that he had had no choice. Even in those less child-centred times a juvenile would not have been questioned without a responsible adult present. The Colonel's frown of displeasure at the intervention was so brief that I almost missed it. But I didn't miss it. I was alive, gloriously alive, to every nuance, every gesture.

I said, 'Saunders is telling the truth, sir. It isn't his. It's mine. He gave it to me before we started out. While we were waiting for Mr Michaelmass.'

'Gave it to you? Why should he do that?' My grand-mother's voice was sharp. I turned towards her.

'He said it was because I'd been kind to Timmy. Timmy is his son. The boys rag him rather.'

The Colonel's voice had changed. 'Was this yo-yo in your possession when Mr Michaelmass fell to his death?'

I looked him straight in the eyes. 'No, sir. Mr Michael-mass confiscated it during the journey. He saw me fiddling with it and asked me how I came by it. I told him and he took it from me. He said, "Whatever the other boys may choose to do, a Charlcourt should know that pupils don't take presents from a servant."'

I had subconsciously mimicked Mr Michaelmass's dry sarcastic tone and the words came out with utterly con-vincing verisimilitude. But they probably would have believed me anyway. Why not? A Charlcourt doesn't lie.

The Colonel asked: 'And what did Mr Michaelmass do with the yo-yo when he'd confiscated it?'

'He put it in his coat pocket, sir.'

The Chief Constable leant back in his chair and looked over at my grandmother. 'Well, that's plain enough. It's obvious what happened. He made some adjustments to his clothing . . .'

He paused, perhaps feeling some delicacy, but my grand-mother was made of tougher metal. She said: 'Perfectly plain. He walked away from Saunders and the boy, not realising that he was dangerously close to the cliff edge. He took off his gloves to undo his flies and stuffed the gloves in his pockets. When he pulled them out again the yo-yo fell. He wouldn't hear it on the snow. Then, disorientated by the darkness, he took a step in the wrong direction, slipped and fell.'

Colonel Neville turned to Saunders. 'It was a stupid place to stop, but you weren't to know that.'

Saunders said, through lips almost as white as his face: 'Mr Michaelmass asked me to stop the car, sir.'

'Of course, of course, I realise that. It wasn't your place to argue. You've made your statement. There's no reason for you to stay on here. You'd better get back to the school and your duties. You'll be needed for the inquest, but that probably won't be for some time. We haven't found the body yet. And pull yourself together, man. It wasn't your fault. I suppose by not saying at once that you'd given the yo-yo to the boy you were trying to protect him. It was quite unnecessary. You should have told the whole truth, just as it happened. Concealing facts always leads to trouble. Remember that in future.'

Saunders said, 'Yes sir. Thank you sir', turned quietly and left.

When the door had closed behind him, Colonel Neville got up from his chair and moved over to the fire, standing with his back to it, rocking gently on his heels and looking down at my grandmother. They seemed to have forgotten my presence. I moved over to the door and stood there quietly beside it, but I didn't leave.

The Chief Constable said: 'I didn't want to mention it while Saunders was here, but you don't think there's any possibility that he jumped?'

My grandmother's voice was calm. 'A suicide? It did cross my mind. It was odd that he told the boy to go over to the boulder and he walked on into the darkness alone.'

The Colonel said: 'A natural wish for privacy, perhaps.'

'I suppose so.' She paused, then went on: 'He lost his wife and a child, you know. Soon after they married. Killed in a car crash. He was driving at the time. He never got over it. I don't think anything mattered to him after that, except perhaps his teaching. My son says that he was one of the most brilliant men of his year at Oxford. Everyone predicted a brilliant academic career for him. And what did he end up by doing? Stuck in a prep school wasting his talent on small boys. Perhaps he saw it as some kind of penance.'

The Colonel asked: 'No relations?'

'None, as far as I know.'

The Colonel went on: 'I won't raise the possibility of suicide at the inquest, of course. Unfair to his memory.

And there isn't a shred of proof. Accidental death is far more likely. It will be a loss for the school, of course. Was he popular with the boys?'

My grandmother said: 'I shouldn't think so. Highly unlikely, I would have said. They're all barbarians at that age.'

I slipped out of the door, still unobserved.

I began to grow up during that Christmas week. I realised for the first time the insidious temptations of power, the exhilaration of feeling in control of people and events, the power of patronage. And I learnt another lesson, best expressed by Henry James. 'Never believe that you know the last thing about any human heart.' Who would have believed that Mr Michaelmass had once been a devoted father, a loving husband? I like to believe that the knowledge made me a better lawyer, a more compassionate judge, but I'm not sure. The essential self is fixed well before the thirteenth birthday. It may be influenced by experience but it is seldom changed.

Saunders and I never spoke about the murder again, not even when we attended the inquest together seven weeks later. Back at school we hardly saw each other; after all, I was a pupil, he a servant. I shared the snobbery of my caste. And what Saunders and I shared was a secret, not a friendship, not a life. But I would occasionally watch him pacing the side of the rugger field, his hands twitching as if there was something he missed.

And did it answer? A moralist, I suppose, would expect us both to be racked with guilt and the new master to be worse than Mr Michaelmass. But he wasn't. The headmaster's wife was not without influence and I can imagine her saying, 'He was a wonderful teacher, of course, but not really popular with the boys. Perhaps, dear, you could find someone a little gentler, and a man we don't have to feed during the holidays.'

So Mr Wainwright came, a nervous, newly qualified teacher. He didn't torment us – but we tormented him. A boys' prep school, after all, is a microcosm of the world outside. But he took trouble with Timmy, giving him special care, perhaps because Timmy was the only boy who didn't bully him. And Timmy blossomed under his loving patience.

And the murder answered in another way – or I suppose you could argue that it did. Three years later the war broke out and Saunders joined up immediately. He was one of the most decorated sergeants of the war, awarded the Victoria Cross for pulling three of his comrades out of their burning tank. He was killed at the battle of El Alamein and his name is carved on the school war memorial, a fitting gesture to the great democracy of death.

And the yo-yo? I replaced it in the box among the school reports, the old essays and those letters from my parents which I thought might interest my son or my grand-children. Finding it, will they briefly wonder what happy childhood memory made an old man so reluctant to throw it away?

Copyright © 1996 by P.D. James

8

THE WESLEYAN
METHOD
Anon. (Attributed to Rik Mayall)

The author is anonymous; the story was first given to the Editor by his gardener, 'Dormy' Woodman, who had heard about Gullible's Travails and made this offering. Actually 'gardener' sounds rather grand. 'Dormy' is an old friend who comes along twice a week and does all the things in the garden which are now beyond the Editor's capabilities, like cutting a large and moss-ridden lawn, flattening the molehills, managing a large bonfire and adding to an even larger compost heap, etc. Anyway, having received 'That's Amazing, Brainians!' from Ben Elton, the Editor was reminded to contact Rik Mayall for a story, for he was then appearing in a re-run of 'The Young Ones' on BBC2, as well as providing the voice-over for 'How To Be a Little Sod' on BBC1, produced by the Editor's son, Jamie. In a friendly and rapid response, Rik submitted a scatological joke which had the Publisher and the Editor reaching for their heart pills – so subsequently allowed his name to be attached to this mildly scatological tale instead. For this we thank him – and 'Dormy'; two for the price of one, in fact – except it was free-of-charge.

A n English lady wished to rent a furnished house in a small German village and, not knowing German, asked for the village schoolmaster to help her.
On her return she remembered that she had not enquired

if there was a W.C. attached to the house. She therefore wrote to the schoolmaster for particulars as to the W.C., but he did not understand the abbreviation, so consulted the Pastor, who also knew a little English. He came to the conclusion that the lady was a devout churchgoer and wished to know where the Wesleyan Chapel was.

He replied to her thus:

Dear Ladyship,

The W.C. is situated 7 miles from your lodgings in the centre of a pine forest in lovely surroundings and open on Tuesdays and Fridays. This is unfortunate if you are in the habit of going regularly, but you will be glad to hear that a number of people take their lunch and make a day of it.

As there are a great number of visitors in the summer, I advise you to go early. The accommodation is good and there are about 80 seats. Should you be late at any time there is plenty of standing space. A bell will ring 10 minutes before the W.C. will be opened. I would especially advise you to go on Tuesdays as on that day there is an organ accompaniment. The acoustics in the premises are excellent, even the most delicate sound being audible all over the building.

My wife and I have been unable to go for some 8 months. It pains us very much but it's such a long way to go. I shall be delighted to reserve the best seat for Your Ladyship and have the honour to be yours etc . . .

9

LAURA NORDER
John Mortimer

The author, both a CBE and a QC, is a barrister who has turned his profession to good account – much to the Great British Public's delight – as a playwright and novelist. In this little tale (which is the copyright of Advanpress Ltd.) he neither employs Rumpole of the Bailey nor takes a voyage round his father. Rather, he considers the case of a man who takes a journey from whose bourn no traveller returns . . .

Little Margery's going to join the battle for Laura Norder – Tim Oldroyd told their friends, when his wife was appointed a magistrate. Law and order was one of his favourite expressions, something he had always 'stood for', but he made it sound as though what he was standing for was a curiously named woman, poor old Laura who was under constant threat from delinquent youth and the anarchist forces of the Party Opposite. When he boasted of his wife's appointment to the minor judiciary it was as though he were announcing a singular and astonishing triumph of his own. As he told her every time the subject was mentioned, which was with embarrassing frequency, she would never have got the job if she hadn't had the good fortune to be the wife of Tim Oldroyd, MP for Boltingly and a Parliamentary Secretary at the Ministry of the Family.

Timothy Oldroyd had been a pallid, shy young man, until some lurking ambition, as hidden up till then as an inherited disease, led him to stand for the seat at Boltingly. A change came over him. He announced that he was now to be known as 'Tim', in the modern way of politicians. He became even paler and grew a paunch and a little sandpaper moustache. His voice, always high-pitched, now emerged as a prolonged whine of outrage. The most frequent objects of his falsetto wrath were school teachers, one-parent families, unemployed school leavers who went joyriding and traded soft drugs in the town's pedestrian precincts, and those who slept in wigwams or up trees in protest at the new eight-lane super highway across Boltingly Meadows. His rage was frequently directed at his wife and then his squeals were weighted with sarcasm and interrupted by moments of light laughter. 'For God's sake, pay attention in court, Margerine!' he told her. 'You know how you tend to let your mind wander. Don't woolgather! The clerk's there to stop you doing anything damn silly. Just get it into your head that, in this country, people don't get stood in dock unless they've committed something fairly outrageous. Support the police and you won't go far wrong. Who's your Chairman?'

'Dr Arrowsmith.'

'Frank Arrowsmith's a wise old bird.' The Oldroyds knew all the important people in Boltingly. 'Listen carefully to what Frank's got to say. Follow his instructions to the letter and you won't go far wrong. I'm sure he won't expect you to make a contribution of any sort. Are you listening, Jerry?'

In fact his wife was staring out of the window at her garden, the lawn she mowed to a soft green velvet and the long border, set against an old brick wall, in which the flowers were all white. The garden, more than anything else in her life, was what kept her with Tim.

'Yes, I'm listening,' she said.

'I don't suppose you've got a suitable hat?'

'I'm afraid not.'

'Pity! In the good old days lady magistrates wore hats. Made them look imposing. That's not your line of country, is it, Margerine? You couldn't look imposing with or without a hat on you.'

From behind the coffee pot, across the polished oval table with its Laura Ashley place mats and Portmeirion breakfast china, Margery Oldroyd looked at her husband and wondered if he'd seem more imposing in a hat, a Princess Di straw perhaps, with an upturned brim and a long ribbon, or a more ornate affair with feathers and artificial roses. How would Tim look, crowned with bobbing cherries like his dreadful mother? This unexpected thought made her giggle.

'And do try not to giggle in court, Margerine.' Her husband issued a serious warning. 'There's a breakdown of respect for all established institutions. As things are today we really can't afford a magistrate who giggles.' With that he left the breakfast table for the lavatory and Bagpiper, the Scottie dog which, in the Oldroyd family, filled, inadequately, the place of a child, rose from the hearthrug and strutted off looking, in its own small way, as superior and discontented as its master.

Margery Oldroyd looked back on twenty-five years of astonishing emptiness. She and Timothy had been at Keele University together. A quarter of a century before, at a party in the J. C. R., when Tim was a skinny student with fairish hair falling into his eyes, she had felt moved by the resolute and purposeful manner, that doomed but bravely undertaken battle against his non-existent sense of rhythm, in which he had tried to dance alluringly to 'I Can't Get No Satisfaction'. She was a sprightly dancer, light on her feet as plump people are, a girl with large surprised eyes, who giggled a good deal. She was attracted by something in Timothy missing in herself, and took it for an infinite ambition: she couldn't guess that it would be so quickly satisfied by becoming a Parliamentary Secretary and the Member for Boltingly. After the J. C. R. dance she led him to her room and steered him towards the bed. When, in a remarkably short time, it was over she smoothed back his straying lock of sandy hair and mistook his incompetence as a lover for sincerity.

Nothing, on that evening, prepared her for the stranger he was bound to become; nor for the alarming intensity with which, she found, she had grown to hate him. This hatred had been born and grew like an advanced and overactive child, even before he started calling her 'Margerine'.

On the magistrates' training course, when they were lectured and questioned on the elements of the law and basic court procedure, Margery had found herself unexpectedly popular. She listened hard, picked up knowledge quickly and showed no signs of giving trouble. Now her first day had come and she was surprised at how calm she felt, far calmer than she had been at breakfast, when her hatred of Tim bubbled up from her stomach and seemed likely to choke her. Now, on the bench, she felt as though she were at a pleasant dinner party to which, she was thankful to say, her husband hadn't been invited. She sat on the Chairman's left. A retired G.P., Frank Arrowsmith had the confidence of a man who, throughout his life, had found it easy to charm women. He may not have been a particularly clever doctor, but he had always been a popular one. Now he sat back at ease in his high-backed, leather-seated chair, listened to tales of distress with a faint smile of amusement and imposed fines or brief terms of imprisonment, in the soft, reasonable voice he had used to recommend a course of antibiotics or a fat-free diet. On the other side of the Chairman sat Gordon Burt, a prosperous garage owner whose skin and clothes hung in greyish folds loosely about his body, giving this squat man, Margery often thought, the appearance of a baby elephant. The first time this comparison had occurred to her she had giggled.

The new Magistrates Court in Boltingly was built of glass and concrete. Inside there was a pervasive smell of furniture polish and disinfectant and the air-conditioning hummed in a soporific fashion. During the first batch of cases Margery's attention wandered. She thought of Tim in his office, accepting coffee from Charlotte, his inevitable researcher. Charlotte, naturally, was everything Margery wasn't, young, slender, intelligent, the possessor of a First in PPE from Lady Margaret Hall, the owner of a 'super little Lotus Elan' which she could drive with skill at speeds Margery could never manage. A girl who, Tim frequently told her, 'knew her opera' as Margery never would, although whether the world of opera belonged to Charlotte and no one else, or if the talented researcher had a private opera of her own, Margery had only once asked, to be met with a look of contempt. Charlotte, she knew perfectly well, was someone to whom Tim made love with greedy haste during lengthy lunch hours or late-night sittings. She would never become Charlie, or even Lottie, although Margery had quickly been demoted to Marge or Jerry, and, for some years now, to Margerine.

'If the bench pleases, may I mention the separation order made in this court?' she heard a solicitor ask in respectful tones, as though from a long way off. Why hadn't she separated from Tim, or even divorced him? He was never tired of telling her that any hint of a broken marriage in the Ministry of the Family would severely 'embarrass the government', as though she cared how embarrassed the government became. When he said this, half threateningly, half in pathetic entreaty, she nursed her ever increasing contempt in silence. Why should she separate from him and move out of the house and away from the garden she loved, to live in a rented flat in Boltingly and haggle over her maintenance, as the couple were going to haggle now in court in front of her? The story of her marriage would, she knew, have some ending, but not that one. So far as Tim Oldroyd MP was concerned, she thought, separation was far too good for him.

'This is the murder,' Dr Arrowsmith smiled and whispered, calling for attention in the way a bridge player might remind her, 'Your deal, partner.' It was the big event in the

Boltingly magistrates' day, R *v* Mustoe, a committal in a murder trial. Margery picked up her pencil and gave the case her full attention.

The man who had been led into the dock, guarded by two prison officers, looked puzzled. He wore jeans and an anorak and he stared around the court as though he wasn't sure of its reality, or whether he was in a dream. He had brown curling hair which he wore rather long and he had, Margery noticed, delicate hands with tapering fingers. He seemed, on the whole, to be taking little interest in the proceedings.

'Mr Mustoe and his common law wife Louise had been separated for some six months. She was living in a mobile home up by Boltingly Meadows and he was sleeping, as he told the officer in charge of the case, "rough". Apparently he had reason to believe she had formed a new relationship with a man working on the new super highway. Er ... Um ...' The young man from the Crown Prosecution Service shuffled his papers nervously and cleared his throat. He looked hot and uncomfortable. What's he worrying about? Margery wondered. This was only a preliminary hearing. He had nothing to do but call a few witnesses to show that there was sufficient case to send up to the Crown Court. Mr Mustoe's solicitor, a lined and yellowing old professional who spent every day in some local criminal court, closed his eyes, leant back and offered no assistance.

'On the night of the 12th April,' the prosecutor resumed uncertainly, 'Mr Mustoe was seen by several witnesses approaching the mobile home. He hammered on the door and was finally let in. Witnesses later heard sounds of quarrelling. We don't know what time Mr Mustoe left but in the morning Louisa Rollins's partner, who had been away for several days, returned and found her dead. The cause of death, you will hear the doctor's evidence, was manual strangulation. Certain fingerprints ...'

'Not admitted!' The old professional boomed without

rising to his feet and the young man from the Crown Prosecution Service subsided meekly.

'Yes?' Dr Arrowsmith raised his eyebrows at the old professional who now rose, his hands clasped together on his stomach and boomed again, 'The fingerprints are not admitted. I shall be cross-examining the officer.'

'But the strangulation,' the retired doctor probed gently. 'Is that admitted?'

'Oh yes, sir. We admit manual strangulation. By *somebody*.'

Gazing vaguely round the court Mr Mustoe, the man accused, caught Margery's eye and, for no particular reason, smiled at her.

'Such amateurs, these criminals! I believe they want to be caught. Why didn't that fellow Mustoe take the precaution of learning a little basic anatomy?' At half past four the committal proceedings were adjourned until the following Monday. Mr Mustoe was remanded in custody and the magistrates retired to their room to enjoy their statutory tea and biscuits before dispersing.

Dr Arrowsmith stretched out his long, well-tailored legs and sipped the watery Lapsang of which he brought his own supply. 'I'm not going to ruin the lining of my stomach with the prison officers' Indian you could stand a spoon up in,' he always said.

'Anatomy?' Mr Burt preferred the local brew. 'How would that help him?'

'My dear Gordon, you might know all about second-hand cars but you'd make a rotten murderer. The carotoid sinus is the place to find. Only a slight pressure needed, it wouldn't leave any bruising you'd notice, and the victim would lose consciousness and be in deep, deep trouble.

'Losing consciousness wouldn't be enough to kill anyone, though. This fellow Mustoe was out to kill her.' Margery watched as the baby elephant spooned sugar into the prison officers' tea.

'Whether the victim came out alive would depend on the

situation she was in. Or he. A small squeeze and they'd be helpless.' The doctor had finished his chocolate biscuit and pulled out a silk handkerchief to wipe his fingers, on the backs of which Margery noticed small clusters of black hair. Hair came out from below his white, gold-linked shirt cuffs also, and encircled his wrist watch. 'Well, anyway,' Mr Burt sounded unconvinced. 'Where are these carotoid whatever they are, anyway?'

'Feel you neck. Gently now. Got the Adam's apple? Now on each side, little swellings . . . the carotoid sinuses.'

Mr Burt stirred his tea as Dr Arrowsmith talked them through it, but Margery's fingers went to her neck, only a little creased by the years since she had been a student and met Tim. Now she had found the exact spot.

'I'm afraid this is rather a morbid sort of conversation for tea time.' The doctor Chairman was smiling at her again. 'No doubt it's a good thing for all of us that the criminal classes are so poorly educated. Now. Let's talk about something far more pleasant. How's your delightful garden, Margery? Don't I remember, when you were kind enough to have Serena and me over to dinner, your lovely white border? What was it that smelled so delicious?'

'That would have been the syringa, I think,' Margery told him. 'Thank you, yes. The garden's still beautiful.'

That night the Oldroyds were invited to a dinner given by the Boltingly Chamber of Commerce, a black tie affair at which Tim was to make a speech and Margery would look up at him admiringly as he painted a rosy picture of the economic situation.

Tim got home early, so he would have plenty of time to change. He was greeted on the stairs by Bagpiper, who appeared embarrassingly affectionate and shot, like a bullet, at his flies. He did his best to calm the dog, then ran himself a bath.

He and Charlotte had enjoyed lunch in an Italian place in Horseferry Road and then retired to a small hotel near Victoria Station, which offered reduced prices for an afternoon. Charlotte was an olive-skinned girl with thick, wiry hair, not as pretty as he would have liked her to be, and she left a musky smell on him which he was anxious to wash away. He cherished the illusion that Margery knew nothing of the way he spent his afternoons.

Tim always enjoyed his bath, and avoided hotels which only offered a shower. He lay back gratefully and turned the tap on with his toe. As the warm water caressed him the years seemed to drift away, and he was back in his student days and he sang, as he once had at a dance, 'I Can't Get No Satisfaction'. The noise of the taps and his singing drowned the footsteps behind him. The strong fingers which closed on his neck were like those of a lover.

Margery had been back to the house earlier. Then she waited, at the end of the garden, until she heard Tim's car. When he had gone upstairs she stood by the back door until she heard the bath water running. 'He's washing off the smell of Charlotte,' was what she said to herself. Then she went shopping in Waitrose, taking care to talk to as many acquaintances as possible. When she returned to the house Bagpiper was kicking up a high-pitched yapping fuss, and water was dripping down the stairs. She turned off the tap and telephoned a Dr Helena Quinton, who had taken over the practice of Dr Arrowsmith, now retired. Then she walked into the garden. The smell of the syringas was sweet and heavy and produced, in her, thoughts of love.

Margery wasn't back in court until the following Monday, for the adjourned hearing of the Mustoe committal. She parked neatly in the space marked 'Magistrates Only' and then went up to their room. Gordon Burt was always late but Dr Arrowsmith was there in excellent time, drinking coffee and eating a digestive biscuit, the chocolate-covered ones were reserved for tea time.

'Margery, dear. I am most terribly sorry.' He stood and spoke very gently, using his best bedside manner.

'Thank you. And thank you and Serena for your note.'

'The funeral's tomorrow, isn't it? We'll be there, of course.'

'That's kind.'

'Helena Quinton said it must have been a sudden heart attack. The poor fellow was unconscious and then drowned. Of course, he'd been overworking terribly. Politics makes such terrible demands nowadays . . .'

'I blame myself.'

'Why on earth?' The doctor's arm was round her shoulder. He was old, too old for work, but he had had, she knew, many mistresses and the smell of eau de cologne on his handkerchief was as strong as the smell of syringas.

'If only I hadn't gone shopping! If only I'd been there in the house, when he came back!'

'That's ridiculous.'

'I felt something was wrong when I was in Waitrose. It must have been a kind of . . .'

'Telepathy?' the wise old doctor suggested.

'Yes.'

'You two were very close. I know you were.' There was a small silence and he squeezed her shoulder. 'We must see more of you now. We mustn't let you be lonely.'

He moved away from her, it seemed reluctantly, when the pachyderm Mr Burt arrived in a hurry. He had also written a note and spoken softly to Margery, as though they were in church together.

'The Mustoe case,' Dr Arrowsmith became business-like now that they were all assembled. 'Now I don't know what we're going to hear today, but the evidence is already overwhelming. I suppose there's no doubt we're sending him for trial?'

'No doubt at all.' Gordon Burt's mouth was half full of digestive biscuit.

'Margery?'

'Oh, Tim always said I was to pay strict attention to what you said and follow your instructions. I must do that, he told me, for the sake of law and order.'

She ran the last syllables together so they sounded like a woman's name, 'Laura Norder'. And as she said it she couldn't suppress a giggle.

10

APRIL IN PARIS?
Brian Rix

The author (Lord Rix of Whitehall CBE, DL), who is also the Editor of this book, now performs at the other end of Whitehall from the theatre which made his name. This tale of an ill-fated trip through the Channel Tunnel provided the catalyst for Gullible's Travails. It also provided the author with a small profit, for all his ticket money was refunded and a return voucher – free of charge – was added. Furthermore, the author hurriedly put pen to paper and sold the saga for publication in the Independent, thus managing, as reported above, an excess of returns over outlay.

Poor Sir Alastair Morton – as Chairman of Eurotunnel has he got problems! Last April he told an astonished financial world that business wasn't too good. Pretty grim, really. Indeed, if I went to bed knowing I had to find £2 million a day just to meet interest payments I don't think I'd sleep much after about 4 a.m. Even Radio 5 Live, Classic FM and the World Service combined would have difficulty in soothing me back into the land of nod.

The trouble is that Eurotunnel has to rely on one or two fairly unreliable partners to make Sir Alastair's dreams come true. Eurostar, for one. Trains running regularly through the tunnel every hour would help its debt

repayments quite a lot. But who ever heard of trains running on time? In this country, anyway.

Two days after Sir Alastair announced those massive losses, I had cause to travel to Paris, via Eurostar, accompanied by my wife and two friends, Tim and Anne. Our objective was to have lunch at the Allard on the Left Bank to celebrate our respective wives' birthdays and then back in time for supper in front of the telly.

Well, that was our objective. The result was far less satisfying. Boarding Eurostar at Waterloo at 7 a.m. – no problem; leaving on time – spot on; but then ... A S-L-O-W journey through the outer reaches of London and the hop fields of Kent, followed by ... a grinding halt. Twenty minutes later came a voice over the PA (with a charming Gallic accent) apologising for the delay – but 'zer were serious troubles with ze power. Zer was none.'

We sat, grimly, facing backwards – if you know what I mean – contemplating the future ahead, locked in a sort of space capsule, with the air conditioning off. From time to time further mentions of 'ze power' or lack of it – wafted over the tannoy but now there was a distinct air of defeatism entering into our conductor's voice, and an equal air of despair entering into the passengers' psyche. When free water was distributed to assuage our, presumed, raging thirsts we began to wonder if we would soon be classed as refugees by the United Nations. At least the loos were working, for we were most certainly not standing in the station.

My friend – Tim – decided to tough it out. Striding up the narrow gangways, sideways, like a demented crab to the front of the train, he bearded the bearded conductor in his den: 'Why can't we go back to Ashford,' he bellowed – convinced that our conductor, being a foreigner, needed a little aural help – 'and we can catch an ordinary train back to London?' Our Gallic conductor was nonplussed by this apparent wisdom. He gabbled furiously into his walkie-talkie, tuned into some off-stage controller at Waterloo station: 'Non, non,' he responded, 'sécurité, sécurité! Pas de personne descend et pas de personne ascend.' Heaven could clearly wait.

My friend decided to pull rank – well, my rank, anyway. 'Mon ami is in Parliament,' he shouted, waving my Rt. Hon. Lord Rix passport, 'he has friends in the Government.'

'We have a member of ze British Cabinet here,' screamed our wild-eyed conductor into his walkie-talkie. 'Yea, yea,' came the response, 'pull the other one.' 'Pull what one?' responded our conductor, thinking – I suppose – of the communication cord. My friend tried a new tack. 'Lord Rix has a heart condition,' he bawled (I have, but it wasn't actually causing any problems at the time), 'he cannot stand the strain any longer and must leave the train immediately.'

Our conductor was not a Frenchman for nothing. Here he was, battling it out in perfidious Albion (well, just outside Ashford, actually) and surrounded by the enemy. 'If he is unwell,' he replied, 'a doctor must be called to certify him.'

Defeated, we retreated to our grim-faced wives and awaited the onward journey, now three hours behind schedule. More life-saving water was distributed – then it was through the tunnel, with no sensation of air pressure at all, just a gentle progression on to Lille, where we were offered release from durance vile and transferred to another capsule returning from Brussels to London. A free meal, grabbed out of yesterday's left-overs from the local deli, I imagine, a glass of warm champagne, grabbed from the same source, and once more through the tunnel. Then the train halted again, nearer Folkestone than Ashford this time, but memories of the morning's incarceration came flooding back as whey-faced returnees exchanged anxious glances. Then we saw it – ze cause of all ze trouble. Shunted into a siding by some good old-fashioned diesel stood the very Eurostar which had lost its electrical connecting rod amongst some overhead cables and blown the whole caboodle. It looked a sorry sight, like a beached Great White with its teeth all drawn. Squatting by it was one engineer viewing some papers on the ground, looking for all the world like Gandhi planning the salt marches, with his bald pate and steel-rimmed glasses glistening in the sun, whilst his three companions appeared a cheerful sight, clad in their bright orange day-glo jackets, but were anything but cheerful as they surveyed the damage above. We stared listlessly at this scene for about a quarter of an hour, then we were off – to be deposited back at Waterloo station eight hours after our departure, with strict instructions that we could apply for a free ticket to Paris before the summer rush.

Summer rush? Poor Sir Alastair. He's relying on that, isn't he? Well, jolly good luck to him, but I think he'll have to overcome a few problems with his partners first. Vehicles on fire, puddles on the tunnel floor, trains without ze power. As for us – we shall always remember the last time we didn't see Paris. The trouble is – so will several hundred others . . .

PART 2

A Voyage to the Americas

1

STARS AT
TALLAPOOSA
William Boyd

The author has written six novels, two collections of short stories and numerous highly successful television and film scripts. He has also scooped up literary awards by the bucketful. He admits to being a singularly untrepid traveller but is occasionally obliged to leave the beaten track in the interests of research, which he does in this tale of touring the American South, searching for the quintessential hick town. He found it – and it emerged in his third novel, Stars and Bars. *The story also appeared in* The Listener *in January 1984.*

It turned out to be a 150-mile detour. Shortly before one o'clock in the afternoon I saw the first sign. 'Welcome to Tallapoosa.' It had an unreal familiarity: Tallapoosa revisited, almost. Then there was another sign. 'Lions Club of Tallapoosa welcomes you. Meets every Thursday at Tally Mt Country Club.' And then, a little way up the road, 'Tallapoosa city limit. Welcome. City of Tallapoosa. Please obey all ordinances. Population 2,869. Drive carefully.' The familiarity, I realised, was a poetic one: 'Stars at Tallapoosa' by Wallace Stevens:

The lines are straight and swift between the stars.
The night is not the cradle that they cry,

The criers, undulating the deep-oceaned phrase.
The lines are much too dark and much too sharp.

The mind herein attains simplicity.
There is no moon, on single, silvered leaf.
The body is no body to be seen
But is an eye that studies its black lid.

'Stars at Tallapoosa' was published in Wallace Stevens's first collection of poems, *Harmonium*, in 1923. It's a perfect example of how he manages to be at once opaque and entrancing. I had read the poem many times and for some reason, when I knew I was going to the South, I looked up Tallapoosa on my Rand McNally road atlas and was disappointed to discover that it was on the Alabama–Georgia border, some considerable distance away from the rough circle of contacts that was going to take me from Atlanta to Augusta, to Charleston, South Carolina, Beaufort, Savannah and back to Atlanta again. My disappointment was mitigated by the consideration that, if I didn't ever get to Tallapoosa, then at least it could be preserved intact in my imagination; that the Tallapoosa Stevens's poem had conjured up for me – the quintessential hick town, but also somehow magic and potent – would never be undermined by reality.

To drive from Savannah to Atlanta you take Interstate 16. It speeds you directly through the rather monotonous countryside that prevails in this corner of Georgia, monotonous because all the trees seem to be of one type – a rather tough-looking average-sized pine. The only relief from this homogeneous landscape comes with each junction or intersection. Here there are gathered the fast-food franchises, the 24-hour supermarkets, the motels, the gas stations. Steak 'n' Ale, Starvin' Marvin, Econo-Lodge, Scottish Inns (the cheapest), Bi-Lo, Wife-Saver, Wife's Nite Off. These huge plastic signs tower high over the countryside, a hundred feet tall, like giant cocktail-stirrers stuck in the earth.

In the big car, a chill cell thanks to the air conditioning, there's nothing to do apart from listen to the radio. Every town has its radio station. You pass them from time to time, a concrete blockhouse below a teetering aerial. I search the wavebands, trying to escape the plangent moralising of country-and-western music, but in vain. If the station isn't broadcasting keening guitars and sobbing voices telling of adultery, divorce, alcoholism, mental and physical cruelty, then it's pumping out religious homilies, sermons and hymns interspersed with advertisements for waterproof Bibles 'for poolside reading' or the Bible on tape 'while you're travelling, working or relaxing at home'.

Macon, Georgia, marks the halfway stage. After the pine forest I was looking forward to Macon – reputedly a grim, featureless industrial town – but Interstate 16 whisked me around it promptly. I was due in Atlanta that evening but had wildly overestimated how long it would take me to get there. By late morning I found I'd covered most of the ground and needed to kill some time. I turned off the highway and drove to a small town called Jackson.

Jackson was nondescript, a typical long, thin town that straggled along the road for a mile or so. A red sandstone courthouse stood in the middle. A notice warned that 'anyone using this building as a comfort station will be prosecuted'. Outside was a cement statue of a soldier. 'Our Confederate Heroes', it said on the plinth.

I went into a café, ordered a Coke and a doughnut and wondered what to do for the rest of the day. I was meandering through the South – Georgia and South Carolina – looking for hick towns, one-horse towns off the beaten track with no touristic allure. I had seen dozens – Smyrna, Bamberg, Denmark, Crawfordville, Madison, Smokes, Apalachee, Walnut Grove, Tyrone. I stopped long enough to mooch around, take some photographs or have a bite to eat. Some were beautiful places, the azaleas blooming fiercely outside immaculate ante-bellum framehouses, the lawns in front of the courthouse and post office cropped like cricket squares, the shops in the malls bright and fresh with new paint. Others were mean and forgotten, consigned to a slow decay and oblivion now that the network of interstate highways so efficiently linked the main centres of population.

In many ways the rural South fulfilled all my expectations. People were poor, attitudes were confined or frozen, and yet I've never encountered such candid friendliness. The first old woman I talked to said, 'Ah do declare', and the Civil War lived on in people's memories as if it had happened only a decade before. But the towns had disappointed me. They were either too frothily perfect – porches, rocking-chairs, coruscating flowers – or drab and banal, lacking any frisson or atmosphere. One caught it occasionally – a group of old black men sitting motionless outside a store in Madison, a shop in Beaufort with a display of trophies from the Little Miss Teenage South Carolina pageant – but it was fleeting or too localised. I wanted something more. I wanted to go to Tallapoosa.

I took out my map and spread it on the table. I was a somewhat alien presence in the café, filled now with Jackson ladies who had interrupted their shopping for a chat. I told myself, not tempting fate, that Tallapoosa would now surely be a smug dormitory for Birmingham or Montgomery, or else have been transformed from what it was in Stevens's day by the erection of some steel mill or sprawling chemical plant, but the urge to see it for myself was too strong to resist. I left Jackson, with its 'comfort station' ban and chattering ladies, with a feeling of elation.

'Tallapoosa city limit. Welcome. City of Tallapoosa. Please obey all ordinances. Population 2,869. Drive carefully.' *City* of Tallapoosa?

The day was hot and the sky cloudless. Soon, on either side of the road, were small wooden bungalows with porches carrying the usual freight of azaleas. At first it all looked too pretty. Then there was a grain silo – a silver cigar – and the houses seemed to fall away as the road climbed quite steeply. Then you hit the brow of the hill and it turns into the main street.

The road is straight. For a hundred yards it runs along-side railway tracks. A railroad running smack through the centre of town, freight trains passing cars in the main street. It looked very strange. I parked the car and got out. Across the tracks was a wide tarmacked area that fronted a modest mall of shops – flat-fronted, two-storey, flat-roofed build-ings. Black cable power-lines, that ubiquitous feature of all American townscapes, looped haphazardly here and there. 'Tallapoosa Drugs' said a big sign above one store. A Coke machine stood outside. The plate-glass window of the shop seemed to contain no items for sale. On the other side of the road were rutted lanes leading to more shops: Talla-poosa Auto, Electrical Goods, Dr Tire, Tallapoosa Seed Merchants, Tallapoosa Home Center. The name was every-where. Tallapoosa Baptist Church.

It was hot and the sun spangled off the railway-tracks and off the windscreens of the large matt and battered cars and pickups parked in front of the mall of shops. There were very few people out and about. Occasionally a car roared through on the way to Bremen down the road, but it was generally very quiet. The town sat low and squat beneath the sun, the pavements were cracked and weeds sprouted freely from the cracks. The fat cars stood squarely on their patches of shadow. I felt no foreboding, only a sense of relief and pleasure.

The mind herein attains simplicity . . .
The body is no body to be seen
But is an eye that studies its black lid.

Let these be your delight, secretive hunter . . .

There certainly was no body to be seen. I stepped up on to the raised wooden sidewalk. On this side of the road, opposite the mall and the railway-tracks, there was a bar. Standing in the doorway behind a mosquito-proofed screen was a man holding a can of beer, wearing dusty denim overalls and a wide, manic smile on his face. I walked by, following the sidewalk to its end. Beyond that there were some sheds, a gas station and an auto shop. Beyond them stretched Alabama and a whole dry country.

The gas station had a small café that operated a drive-thru window. Three cars were parked outside. In each, two women sat in the front and children lounged in the back. Everybody was eating. A girl hung out of the drive-thru window, talking to the women in one of the cars.

As I approached, they stopped talking and turned and looked at me. I changed course, crossed the street, stepped tentatively over the thick, burnished railway-tracks, through a strip of knee-high, sun-bleached grass and weeds, and on to the broiling parking-lot in front of the mall. Dusting my trouser legs free of seeds and grass burrs. I saw the red neon rosette of a Budweiser sign glowing palely in the sunlight. Bars at Tallapoosa. I went in.

It was very dark. And full of men – white men. Drunk men.

A long bar stretched back into the depths of the room where there was an antiquated mechanical skittle-machine. Dusty plastic beer signs advertised Millers, Budweiser, Pabst. There were racks of old bottles of what I took to be country wines. A hand-printed sign said 'No credit. No personal checks', but some drunken good ol' boy was loudly trying to persuade the taciturn, impassive barman to break his own house rules.

I asked politely for a beer and was given one in the can. Looking around, I saw that everyone drank direct from the bottle or the can. There wasn't a glass in sight. I stood there, one hand in one pocket, and tried to drink my beer as fast as possible. No one spoke to me or showed the slightest curiosity. They were just waiting patiently for me to get my drinking done and get out. I didn't belong here, I was an irritant in the melancholy life of the bar. When I put my empty can down, the barman muttered the obligatory Southern valediction, 'Y'all come back and see us again some time, heah?', but his heart wasn't in it.

Outside I was dazzled by the glare of the sun. Then I saw

a big maroon car cruising very slowly through the mall. A girl was driving and another sat beside her in the front. It slowed to a crawl as it passed the bar. The girls – 18 going on 30 – were smoking and had dyed blond hair. The car had a hub-cap missing. It looked too big for the girls to drive. I let it pass and walked across the car park, stepped back over the railway-lines and across the main street. The car pulled out of the mall, bumped across the tracks and accelerated away in the direction of Bremen. The girls were laughing at something.

> Their pleasure that is all bright-edged and cold . . .
> Making recoveries of young nakedness.

The town seemed stuck in its hot midday stupor. Where was everybody? I wondered. In the bars? I walked down towards the white Baptist church, wooden, painted white. The Baptists have Georgia sewn up. I saw a pawn shop and next door another drugstore. I went in, hoping to find a soda fountain or some kind of snack-bar but with no luck. Instead, I bought another reel of film from the little moustachioed man who worked inside. He asked me where I was from. I told him. He said, maybe to make me feel less of a stranger, that there were two or three European girls who lived in Tallapoosa; German girls who had married Tallapoosa men serving in Germany and who had been brought back to the States to live. I wondered what the German girls must have made of their new home. The promise of a new life in the USA. The reality of a lifetime in Tallapoosa.

I asked the little man if there was a nice restaurant in town where I could get a bite to eat. He thought for a while – it was clearly something of a poser – and said that I should head out of town on the road to Bremen; then turn left, following the signs for Interstate 20. There was 'quite a decent little place' about two miles down that road.

I followed his instructions. Turning off the Tallapoosa–Bremen road, I saw a large factory: the Tallapoosa Rubber

Company. Perhaps its presence explained the paucity of men on the streets. I drove on, looking for the restaurant. Then I saw it: the 'Big O' hamburger house, on the Tallapoosa exit of Interstate 20. So this was the best restaurant in town.

Inside it was empty, not a solitary trucker. Greasy formica, battered, chipped chairs, drab curtains. The 'Big O' offers that day were Mountain Man stew and steak sandwiches. I chose a steak sandwich.

Two bored girls took my order. They looked like younger sisters of the girls in the car: heavy make-up, streak jobs, glinting jewellery. My sandwich came – a small steak fried in batter, a leaf of iceberg lettuce and a squirt of mayonnaise. I hankered vaguely for Mountain Man stew.

I ate my sandwich and thought about Tallapoosa. It had been the evocativeness of the poem that had lured me here. But in my reading I had imagined something entirely different from the banalities of small-town America. Now the lines between the stars were merely the haphazard loopings of electric cable spanning the street and alleyways. The stars themselves were reduced to sunbursts off windscreens and dusty chrome. To a significant extent the topography of the poem is redundant – no doubt Stevens never expected any reader to check it out. Its power resides in the potency of its phrase-making: 'secretive hunter', 'recoveries of young nakedness', 'the lost vehemence the midnights hold'. And yet it wasn't all disappointment. Even though I had no idea what Wallace Stevens was doing in the place, I sensed an understanding, some fifty years or more later, of the entrancement he seemed to have felt, or at least a rendered-down, displaced 1980s version. Tallapoosa was so tawdry and down-at-heel and yet here, undeniably, I had found the very frisson I was after, that formed a bridge, albeit a flimsy one, between the experience of the poem and the reality of the present. The atmosphere on the main street had been a kind of brazenness, a flashiness, a self-confidence manifested in the constant reiteration of the name: Tallapoosa this, Tallapoosa that.

Perhaps it was the name alone that had attracted Stevens – some incantation in its utterance that infected the citizens and the environment. Or was I merely wishful-thinking, investing the place with my personal designs on it, my eye studying its own black lid?

I left the 'Big O' and drove back to take some more photographs. I wandered uneasily around, snapping shots covertly. The girls in the maroon car were back, parked at the drive-thru, eating something, but the streets were as quiet as ever.

> Let these be your delight, secretive hunter,
> Wading the sea-lines, moist and ever-mingling,
> Mounting the earth-lines, long and lax, lethargic.
> These lines are swift and fall without diverging.
>
> The melon-flower nor dew nor web of either
> Is like to these. But in yourself is like:
> A sheaf of brilliant arrows flying straight,
> Flying and falling straightway for their pleasure.
>
> Their pleasure that is all bright edged and cold;
> Or, if not arrows, then the nimblest motions,
> Making recoveries of young nakedness
> And the lost vehemence the midnights hold.

I didn't stay to see the stars at Tallapoosa. I left for Atlanta long before night fell.

2

A HITCHHIKER'S GUIDE
TO THE ANDES
Miles Kington

The author first came to the Editor's attention when he was playing double bass for the musical group Instant Sunshine, which consisted of three doctors and the humorous columnist himself; the Editor (then a theatrical producer) engaged the highly amusing quartet to entertain the theatre-going public in the totally unsuitable, cavernous Shaftesbury Theatre. In spite of all the odds, the group were very entertaining and attracted reasonable audiences, having come from a much smaller venue at the Edinburgh Festival. The author is also very entertaining and better known, perhaps, for his regular, witty articles in the Independent (and before that, in The Times) and here tells a story in which our hero breaks down with a broken axle 12,000 feet up in the Andes and tries to hitch a lift at midnight in guerrilla country with only a toy llama to keep him warm.

In 1980 I went with a BBC TV team to Peru to film the highest railway line in the world which starts at sea level and goes up to the top of the Andes, though film crews much prefer to lug their stuff about by car whenever possible, rather than get on a train and mix with the public, who might well nick their things. In any case, there is only one passenger train a day up the Andes, as I found to my cost when doing the recce trip – the train broke down about

10,000 feet up in the mountains, and whereas in Britain we might wait for another train to come along, the Peruvians know that there won't be another train along until tomorrow, and all the passengers got off the train and started walking to the nearest village for lifts home, and so did I after a while . . .

So I wasn't too unhappy to go about the country by car, especially as there is a good road from Lima up the Andes and over the top. We were coming back down this road at midnight, at the end of shooting, when I discovered a vital truth I hadn't known before; in Peru, you give way to vehicles that are bigger than you.

The way we discovered this was through a lorry that came up the road towards us in the middle of the road. We drove down towards him, waiting for him to get over to his side. Too late our assistant cameraman, who was driving, realised that the lorry driver wasn't going to get over and, just to avoid death, drove into the verge. There was a loud bang. The car stopped. We got out. It was very dark, but not so dark that we couldn't see the concrete culvert into which we had driven and broken the back axle.

There was a voice coming out of the culvert. It was saying, in English: 'Get me out of here!' It belonged to our sound man, who had just fallen into it in the dark, and later testified that it was about ten feet deep.

The car belonged to Avis Rentacar of Lima. Lima was about two hundred miles away, and we thought the offices would probably be closed at midnight, even if we had a phone. We didn't have a phone. There was no human habitation in sight. It was very dark and very cold and very high up and very quiet. I had never been in this situation before. But I knew that film crews are always getting into scrapes.

'What do we do now?' I said.

'Well,' said John Howarth, the cameraman, 'we hitch a lift back to Lima.'

There hadn't been a vehicle on the road since the lorry had forced us off.

'Who with?' I said.

'Got a better idea?' he asked.

A lorry stopped for us about an hour later, going down the road to Lima, carrying potatoes, heading for the fruit and veg market. There was room in the cab for two passengers. There were four of us. There were already two passengers in the cab. The driver said, in sign language, that if we wanted to lie on top of the potatoes, it was fine by him. The four of us threw the film equipment up there and climbed up on top of the potatoes and made ourselves as comfortable as you can on top of a few tons of potatoes.

It was, in a way, suitable that we had been rescued by a potato lorry, because potatoes are one of the two things which Peru is famous for originating. The other is llamas. I had a llama with me. It was about three feet long and stuffed, and I was taking it home as a souvenir. But now I had a better use for it; as a pillow.

'I can't get to sleep,' said a small voice next to me an hour later. It was the production assistant, the only girl out of the four of us. I hadn't realised till that moment that any of us were trying to get to sleep. When you're lying on your back in the freezing Andes on a precarious potato lorry ten feet above the ground and travelling at speed, sleep is not the first thing you think of.

'Have my llama,' I said kindly.

And she did, and using it as a pillow she dropped off to sleep, and I lay awake for hours, staring up at the stars which I had never seen so bright before in all my life and wishing I had brought my *Daily Telegraph* map of the heavens which used to hang on my bedroom wall, and wishing I could get to sleep, but not daring to drop off in case I fell off, but I must have done somewhere along the road because just as the dawn was breaking, not far from Lima, there was another big bang and the lorry stopped.

'Puncture,' said the driver ruefully.

We found a phone and rang Lima. Avis was still not open, so we got the producer out of his hotel bed in Lima and made him drive out to get us. The lorry driver was still having trouble with his puncture.

'Want a lift?' we said to him, when the producer arrived.

'Only if you can take the potatoes as well,' he said.

I can't say that it was a desperate experience, all in all, but I have never complained about any mattress since. Anything is better than potatoes.

3

HISTORY OOZES
FROM EVERY STONE
IN THE PLACE
Bernard Levin

*The author, one of the most acclaimed and original journalists of
our time, is renowned as a columnist for* The Times, *as a music
buff, a theatre critic, a defender of lost causes – which he often
turns into winning ones – and as a man with a razor wit who
has written millions of splendid words for a variety of publi-
cations and programmes. In this visit to Santa Fe, New Mexico,
he explores the musical traditions of this fascinating – but often
chilly – town. The exploration first took place in 'Pleasures' on
Radio 3 in 1981.*

Santa Fe has a fair claim to the title of the oldest town
in the United States, and the undisputed possession
of America's oldest church and oldest house. But it is
not just its antiquity that makes this place, with a population of barely 50,000, so remarkable; Santa Fe has lived
through history, but has also made it, and in very substantial quantities. The Palace of the Governors has housed a
succession of rulers; what makes it unique in the United
States is that it has been the local administrative head-
quarters of *three* mighty powers. For two centuries this was
the watchtower for the northernmost marches of the Spanish empire in the Americas; when Mexico threw off Spanish
dominion, Santa Fe became the centre of government for

the new rulers; and since 1848 it has been the capital of, first, the Territory, and then the State, of New Mexico.

History oozes from every stone in the place. The adobe architecture is still the only kind permitted in the town centre, and some of the ways in which modern architects have adapted themselves to it are most imaginative. My first glimpse of the Loretto Inn caused me to start back with a yelp, struck by the dismaying thought that Le Corbusier had come to life again, madder than ever; but when I saw, after walking about the town a little, how this strange building echoes and varies the ancient theme, I understood what its builder had been aiming for, and also, I think, why Santa Fe is so proud of its past and of the visible marks that that past has left.

The low, smooth walls, with the crossbeams projecting through them to the outside: the window apertures that look as though they were punched out with a biscuit-cutter in the wet clay: the sunset glow that the tinted facing gives off: this truly makes Santa Fe a rose-red city, half as old as time.

But the reminders of what has happened in that time are everywhere, and some of them have struck deep roots. The heart of the city is a green oasis called the Plaza; in the centre stands a simple obelisk, commemorating those who fell in the wars that raged back and forth across this area. One side is dedicated 'To the heroes who have fallen in the various battles with Indians in the Territory of New Mexico', but before the word 'Indians' there is a blank space, from which, it is clear, another word has been gouged out with a chisel. The word was 'savage'; the inscription had originally referred to 'savage Indians'. I turn my head an inch, and I can see the frontage of the Palace of the Governors, running right along one side of the Plaza. Beneath the portico sits a continuous row of Indians, come to town to sell their wares – necklaces, pottery, leather; inside the museum that the Palace of the Governors now houses there are Indian artefacts going back to the eleventh century; everywhere in this town those proud, axe-like profiles can be seen. Whoever plied the chisel on the monument had a better, or at any rate a longer, sense of history than whoever put it up.

New Mexico is the third poorest state in the Union; only Alabama and Mississippi are worse off. The countryside provides evidence of the bare living which the pioneers scratched from a miserly soil, and which their descendants scratch still. Scorched hillsides, dotted with scrubby bushes, miniature pines and junipers, rise from the desert plains; fragments of ghost towns, long abandoned, are strewn across the landscape; inside the historical museum we learn how a people with no metal of their own and no opportunity to import it still found ways to survive, and passed on that survival instinct to those who came after. A European visitor to Santa Fe would do well, as soon as he has got his bearings, to stop and reflect upon the fact that the first American to show his face there did so as late as 1805, that the first trail along which wagon-wheels could roll was opened in 1828, and that the standard means of exchange was barter, not currency, until late in the nineteenth century.

The European visitor, however, is much more likely to be struck by the fact that Santa Fe has a larger number of art galleries, for its population, than any other place on earth: on the same scale, London would have 15,000. One long street, indeed, the delightful Canyon Road, is almost entirely composed of them, and there are arcades more throughout the city. Santa Fe has no industry to speak of (the historical area has no neon lighting, either – it's forbidden), and must live on tourism, but that alone would not account for the way in which it seems to have added the galleries of Bond Street to those of St Ives and multiplied by the number it first thought of.

Over the years, like immigrants who huddle together in the same district for comfort against the strangeness of a new country, more and more artists have found in Santa Fe and the surrounding countryside inspiration, peace and – by no means the least important – exceptionally good light.

After the painters and sculptors came the poets and novel-
ists (D. H. Lawrence settled near by), and by the end of the
Second World War Santa Fe was renowned as a centre of
artistic endeavour and achievement. (There is even a street
called Artists Road.)

But one of the arts was missing; no musical tradition had
grown up alongside those of words and images. Well, we
all know, or we should do by now, what America does
when she discovers a lack of tradition: she turns to and
creates one overnight. And that, almost literally, is what
happened in Santa Fe. John Crosby, a musician in New
York, had spotted the gap in the cultural life of this cultured
city, and from discussions with a group of his colleagues
an idea was born.

Cunningly concealed just behind the Santa Fe Opera
House there is a beautifully laid out estate, its lawns and
flowerbeds offering a hint of Glyndebourne; in this area,
part of the ten-acre ranch site originally bought by Crosby,
the musicians both work and disport themselves, and here,
too, are the administrative offices of the Opera. It was here
that I talked to Crosby, and where he explained the idea to
me. In those days, not long after the war, the opportunities
among American musicians for work in the summer were
very limited, and providing such opportunities was a large
part of the plan. That may sound like putting the stagecoach
before the horses, but in the ears of players and singers
accustomed to being laid off throughout the summer it
must have sounded like the invitation to the waltz.

The plan, of course, was to build an opera house in the
foothills of the Sangre de Cristo mountains, which are more
or less in the middle of the desert, and there stage an
annual summer festival of opera, running a full two
months. And that is what they did; John Crosby was its
Director when it opened in 1957, and he is still its director,
and chief conductor, in this its Silver Jubilee year. The
original theatre held only 460 people; it was burned to the
ground in 1967 (the cause of the fire has hitherto remained
unknown, although – as you shall hear – I have now solved

the mystery) and promptly rebuilt on a much larger scale, for, by then, a decade after the festival had been founded, it was clear that the Santa Fe Opera had captured the imagination of America's music-lovers. The new house, an affair of handsome criss-cross, sweeping curves, holds 1,800 and is filled to more than 90 per cent of its capacity throughout the season.

This is especially remarkable because, from the start, the Santa Fe Opera has specialised in operatic rarities, and most particularly in new works, some of them specially commissioned or works new to the United States; the composers represented in these categories include Berg, Berio, Henze, Hindemith, Penderecki, Schoenberg, Shostakovich and Villa-Lobos – none of them exactly guaranteed to provide queues at box offices. Though, on the other hand, as Crosby pointed out to me, a large proportion of Santa Fe audiences are opera fanatics who come there precisely in order to see operas they cannot see elsewhere; and I must admit that I have been vainly seeking a stage performance of Richard Strauss's *Daphne* for most of my musical life, to be rewarded at last by stumbling upon it at the end of the Old Santa Fe Trail. (It is, incidentally, a work of ravishing beauty, with much of Strauss's finest music, and why it has not held the stage like *Salome* and *Elektra* – it is far superior to both of them – I cannot imagine, especially after seeing it in this penetrating production by Colin Graham, who was not afraid to let his characters keep still and pour out the golden stream of melody and feeling.)

But, before that, I had to be initiated into the experience of opera in Santa Fe; the first work I saw after my arrival was *La Bohème*. As it happens, it wasn't much of a *Bohème*, but I tell you that, if the hero and heroine had been sung by Caruso and Callas, with Toscanini conducting, I would have found it impossible to enjoy the performance, or indeed to pay more than occasional attention to it, so frightful, so unspeakable, so utterly without precedent in all my years of opera-going in a score of countries and upwards of fifty houses, were the conditions under which it was given.

The Santa Fe Opera House is an open-air one; that is, it is completely open on both sides, and the shell which curves out over the stage and pit falls short of meeting the opposite shell, over the balcony, by eight rows of the stalls. In the afternoon it had begun to rain, steadily, copiously and mercilessly, while the temperature had fallen concomitantly to the level of a cold late-October day in London. As I went to my place (it was beneath the covered section) I saw the patrons of rows K to S bailing pints of water out of the concave seats – nobody even thinks to put tarpaulins over them when it rains – preparatory to sitting down and catching pneumonia. The wise, whether accommodated in the quick-suicide area or the slow-murder, had come suitably dressed; throughout the house there were quilted anoraks, all-enveloping waterproof capes, scarves, galoshes, blankets and rugs, balaclava helmets, fur hats with ear-flaps, muffs, *and umbrellas.*

Covered seats or uncovered, none of it was of the smallest avail; the cold and damp bored into our bones, numbing the body and the senses alike. At the first interval I fled up the steps in search of a roof and walls, to discover that there aren't any. There is no lobby, no foyer, no snack bar, no marquee; the very drink is sold in the open air, and there is not even a covered way to the washrooms. Well, at least the mystery of the blaze which destroyed the previous Santa Fe opera house is cleared up: it was obviously set on fire by some poor devil trying to keep warm.

Things got better – if they hadn't, you would not be listening to me now, and an English coroner would, I trust, be saying some sharp things about John Crosby. Next day it was almost as cold, but at least dry; and for the last two operas I saw, the nights could without mockery have been described as pleasant. And so could the performances: there was a sumptuous and exciting production of Hindemith's *News of the Day*, a humorous trifle not nearly so ponderous as I had feared, and very well sung, particularly by Mary Shearer and James Atherton; and, finally, the one unqualified success of the festival, *The Rake's Progress,* directed by Bliss Hebert and conducted by Raymond Leppard. Leppard dug deep beneath the brilliance of the surface to find the passion, irony and regret in this tremendous score; Hebert's direction was full of imagination and understanding; and the performance of Nick Shadow by James Morris would grace any opera house in the world.

But there are two music festivals in Santa Fe, not one. And it is at the other one – which consists entirely of chamber music – that, for the first time since I started this tour, I have heard performances which have *consistently* been of the very highest international standard, with no allowances or qualifications required. The Santa Fe Chamber Music Festival is very much the younger of the two: it is nine years old, to the Opera's twenty-five. And it is not as long: it lasts five weeks, to the Opera's eight, though as against that I was astonished to discover that practically all the concerts are repeated twice elsewhere – first in Seattle, immediately after the end of the performances in Santa Fe, and then in New York.

There are links with the other arts in the chamber music festival, too. In its first year they approached Georgia O'Keeffe, one of America's finest painters, now 94 years old but still working, to ask if they might reproduce for the poster advertising the festival one of her pictures, which are full of the landscapes and atmosphere of this part of the United States. She readily agreed and, each year since, she has selected a painting and offered them the use of it; this year's, indeed, binds three of the arts together, for it is entitled *The Lawrence Tree*. This year she has also lent them one of her sculptures, a beautiful, shell-like form which stands upon the platform in the hall where most of the concerts take place.

The intensity and devotion that the musicians bring to their work here reminded me of Rudolf Serkin's Marlboro, where I started this musical voyage, and I was not surprised to learn that many of the Santa Fe players – they come back year after year – are themselves Marlboro 'graduates'. One of the features of the chamber music festival is a weekly open rehearsal, in which not only the musicians but also the audience discuss and comment on the music and its performance. And every year they have an American composer-in-residence, from whom they commission one or more works for performance in the course of the festival, and who also leads further public discussions of the writing, playing and listening to music.

Out of all this I have heard, not only a fine piano quintet by this year's Santa Fe composer, John Harbison (he teaches music at the Massachusetts Institute of Technology, where I imagine they need music more than any other place on earth), full of staccato rhythms and long, lyrical passages, but some playing of more familiar works that has been the equal of anything I have ever heard. A very young violinist and pianist, Daniel Phillips and Andras Schiff, gave a dazzling performance of Dvorak's Sonatina, Op. 100, and Heiichiro Ohyama, accompanied by Edward Auer, played a Bach sonata for viola da gamba in a manner that could hardly have been surpassed by Zukerman and Barenboim. And on my last night I heard a concert consisting of three masterpieces played by virtuosos: the Mozart Clarinet Quintet, in a performance of exquisite tenderness; Schoenberg's *Verklärte Nacht*, with all its astounding romanticism caught and held; and the *Dumky* Trio of Dvorak, a work like a Catherine wheel with the Cheshire cat's grin, played – by Edward Auer, Yuuko Shiokawa and Timothy Eddy – for all the fire and wit it is crammed with.

Under the spell of such pure music – and, to be fair, under the spell also of the beauty of Strauss's *Daphne* and the performance of *The Rake's Progress* – I can almost persuade myself that I dreamed the rain and the cold on the night of *La Bohème*, and even the exceptional vileness of the coffee they serve at the opera house. Besides, I have now heard the Mozart Clarinet Quintet on two successive Sundays; and in Santa Fe's Museum of the American Indian I have seen a teepee ('wigwam', it seems, is a misnomer) 15 feet high, for which any small boy would sell his soul, or even his collection of marbles, to Nick Shadow; and I have eaten the chili-laden Mexican cuisine and survived; and I have seen the Miraculous Staircase in the Chapel of Our Lady of Light.

This spiral staircase, up to the choir loft, makes two complete 360-degree turns in seven yards of height, and has no central pillar or support, being held in place only by the perfection of its making; for that matter, it has no nails anywhere in it. But the grace and delicacy of its beauty, as it seems to float, not climb, from the chapel floor to the balcony, is like no other creation I have ever seen from the hands of a craftsman, and would itself have made the journey to Santa Fe worthwhile.

It is called the Miraculous Staircase because of the circumstances in which it was built. The workmen, in 1878, had abandoned the building of the chapel at this point, saying that it was impossible to fit a staircase in. A stranger appeared in the town, volunteered for the job, completed it in six months, and disappeared without either giving his name or asking for payment. It is certainly a miracle in the colloquial sense; the Sisters, of course, believed that it was a real miracle, and certainly no visitor who looks upon it, and has heard the story, can fail to think of one particular carpenter. True, this is a piece about music festivals, not theology. All the same, I cannot help remarking that if the Sisters were right, and the stranger *was* that carpenter, it is hardly to be wondered at that he would not hammer nails into wood.

4

FROZEN IN TIME
Brian Rix

The author has the temerity, as Editor, to add this postscript to Bernard Levin's visit to Santa Fe. The Editor, too, has frozen in that place for, as indicated by Mr Levin, it can be very cold. In this little story, musical matters of a considerably lighter kind than those experienced by the great diarist were being discussed. After all, Jack Good did originate 'Oh Boy' in the good old R & R days on television, as well as compiling the award-winning musical Elvis, *along with Ray Cooney – but by the time of this tale he was very much part of the Santa Fe artistic scene. This piece was originally published in the second part of the Editor's autobiography,* Farce About Face.

I must tell you the story of a trip to Santa Fe, when Ray Cooney, his wife Linda and I went over to discuss all manner of musical matters with Jack Good: *Elvis*, 'Oh Boy', and a new idea for the life story of Bing Crosby, which never came to anything. An alternative, *Music, Music, Music*, was suggested by Jack, but that never came to anything either.

Anyway, after Jack, Ray and I had banged our heads against a brick wall for three or four days, Jack's wife Margit (she was born in Germany and christened Margrit, but the priest missed out the second 'r', so Margit she

remains) suggested that we repair to the nearby Indian Reservation, which encompassed holy ground. We pointed out that it was now 4.30 in the afternoon and the Reservation closed at 5.00, but Margit persisted. We clambered into the VW van and lumbered off.

At the Reservation gates we were greeted by a somewhat startled Red Indian gatekeeper, who pointed out that the whole place, spirits and all, closed up at five o'clock and it was now ten minutes to. Margit was German in the extreme. 'We will be back by five o'clock precisely,' she declaimed – and we were off.

It seems to me that all Red Indians must have been four feet tall or squatted permanently on their hunkers, for the ruins on the holy ground indicated rooms of four foot two inches by four foot two inches (4'2" × 4'2" – for those of you who find numerals easier to follow) with no room to stretch for a reasonable-sized dog, never mind a human.

By now, dusk was falling and it was extremely cold. I glanced at my watch. 'Oh my God,' quoth I, 'it's ten past five.'

'Have no fear,' responded Margit, 'those Indians will wait for us.'

They didn't. The whole place was firmly secured to keep us in and to keep all intruders out. Even though the living had to adhere to normal working hours, there was no intention of the spirits being disturbed during the night watches – though they might have been working in twenty-four-hour shifts. So there we were. Secure within an Indian Reservation. The great American Dream locked irredeemably outside.

We contemplated the heavily bolted gate. No way. We inspected the barbed-wire entanglements which bordered it. Even worse. We were stuck. And all we had to live in (or sleep in) was a clapped-out old Volks with enough holes in the body to let the icy blasts blow through it like a colander. We could well freeze to death on a New Mexican hillside.

It was no use rounding on our hostess, Margit, with

KLM
Check-in - Büro
Abflughalle
Flughafen Frankfurt
6000 Frankfurt/Main

Germany

Herzliche Grüße aus dem
schönen Kanada. Vielen, vielen
Dank für die freundliche Hilfe
beim Wiedereinfangen von 'Ervin'
und der schnellen, unkomplizierten
Erledigung der Formalitäten!

Alles Gute   Bettina Sochan

accusations of Teutonic arrogance. It was no good cursing the Red Indian gateman for being a lazy, good-for-nothing bastard. We might join the spirits in this place if we didn't do something pretty fast.

Ray and I returned to the VW. We inspected what was laughingly known as the tool-box, and came forth with a jack and a tyre wrench. Placing the jack under the left-hand side of the gate, we literally forced the hinges apart, by the simple expedient of jacking the gate up and wrenching the metal away as it gradually succumbed to fatigue. We could now swing the gate open, using the central post as the fulcrum.

But Indian Reservations have strange guardians. As we delighted in our ingenuity and the gate came swinging free, we saw the biggest bull you have ever seen, glowering at us, with head lowered, from the free ground. We hastily leaned the gate back and convened a council of war.

We decided that Margit would edge the VW up to the gate, Ray and I would swing it ajar, Linda would open the back doors of the van, Margit would block the opening as best she could and Ray and I would sprint for safety – leaping into the van as it swept through the jacked-open gate.

It worked! But as we drove through, Running Bull decided to charge, ending up inside the Reservation. Ray and I leapt out of the van, propped the gate up against its original post and, breathing a collective sigh of relief, we drove off into the freezing night air to the nearest bar and several tequilas.

We wished we could have been there in the morning. The Red Indian gatekeeper arriving – unlocking the central part of the gates – trying to swing them open – the left-hand gate falling on his foot and Running Bull charging him, all at the same time.

That'll teach the Red Indians to cross a German Squaw.

5

A NIGHT OUT
IN LLAMAC
Matthew Parris

The author, also described as a journalist and broadcaster, was once the Conservative MP for West Derbyshire. Now, however, he confines his political sallies to a pungent, perspicacious piece – daily – in The Times, *as well as broadcasting his views and comments over the airwaves, both visual and aural. This piece has been published by Phoenix in the author's book* Inca-Kola, *as well as appearing in* Views from Abroad: 'The Spectator' Book of Travel Writing, *published by Grafton. In spite of these previous airings, the story will come as a surprise to most readers, who will be expecting a light-hearted romp but will be rather taken aback to find their inherent fears of the dark (and foreign parts) described only too well . . .*

S eeing Nazario and his relatives was like coming home. They brought us a drink of hot water with sugar in it, and Nazario confided that they had doubted even whether we would get beyond the lake. They had not expected Mick to return on his feet.

Had we heard about the New Zealanders? Apparently a New Zealander and his Israeli girlfriend had been killed on Yerupaja. His mother, who was South African, was waiting in Chiquian for the body.

It was a lively homecoming, with much exclaiming,

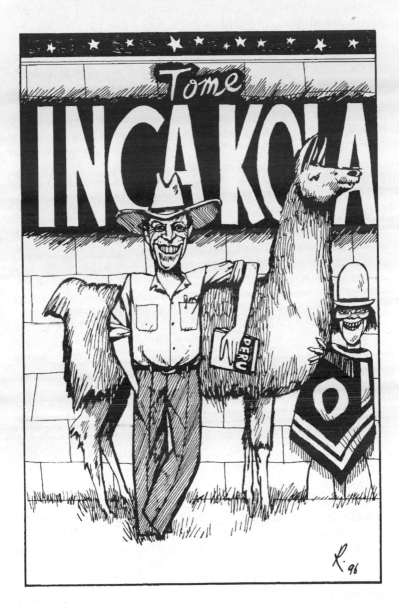

many questions and a few tall stories. Rested and refreshed, we asked Nazario whether there was a bar in Llamac, and whether he would have a drink with us there.

'Yes,' he replied, rather hesitantly. 'There is a bar called La Venta. But are you sure? Are you sure I should come?' Obviously the high life was not something he was used to.

We had seen this village, first, as a high outpost – smaller and more remote than anywhere we had been before. Now it was different. Llamac was the big city, the king of all the little settlements and villages we had been passing through during our days in the mountains beyond. There, people spoke of Llamac as one might of Babylon or Kansas City. The timid and the infirm had never been here. There was even a bar.

So now it looked different – busy, prosperous, boasting the two-storey houses and tin roofs that were the envy of lesser villages. Here there was a water-borne sewage system – water coursing down gulleys in the centre of the main alleys. Here there were not just burros and mules, but horses tethered outside. Here there were transistor radios – though, unfortunately, a shortage of batteries – children singing, and pigs and ducks in the road.

It was late, for Llamac, by the time we reached the La Venta. It seemed to be shut. Nazario had come with us after much urging on our part, and much doubting, on his, whether he should. We guessed that he did not normally drink.

He knocked hesitantly at the wooden door, then rattled it violently when there was no response. The proprietor opened up, in a nightshirt. We would have apologised and left, but he was insistent, so in we went.

It was pitch dark. Our host lit two candles and fetched beer. Nazario did not know how to pour his, and spluttered violently after his first mouthful. We sat, talking, the candles guttering, and the proprietor gazing benignly on, delighted not so much by Ian's taking of a photograph as by the flash, which he had never seen before.

Mick told us about his journey down, with Carlos and

his younger brother, Flavio – how Carlos had shinned up a tree to rob a dove's nest but come down empty-handed. 'Only one hatched. I left them. I will return in a few days when the young chicks are ready to eat. *Palomitas tiernas* (tender little chicks)!' – and how Carlos and his brother had quizzed him continuously about life over the seas, but in particular about how long people lived in Europe and America. This question seemed to fascinate them.

Nazario was becoming quite animated. A glass of beer was going rather to his head, and he kept shaking hands with each of us in turn.

'Do they have bandits in Europe?' he asked, apropos of nothing much.

'Not as many as Peru,' I replied.

'You have met them here?'

'Not this time, but three years ago.'

The others groaned. They knew what was coming.

'Tell me! Tell me!'

'Go on then, Matt. Tell him. I'll translate. *Again.* It's beyond your Spanish. The others can talk among themselves.' So, with Mick translating, I began.

We were three friends: Luisa (an Italian interpreter from Luxembourg), Francis and I.

A Social Democrat candidate for the European Parliament, Francis was taking a holiday before hitting the campaign trail in Hampshire. Once his inevitable defeat had taken place, he planned to write a book about European political parties. It was my first time in Peru, Luisa's first time camping, and Francis's first time high-altitude trekking.

The story begins as we came to the end of a long day's march in the mountains somewhere between Puno and Cuzco. Following the little Rio Tigre towards its source, high in the Andes, we had steadily gained altitude all day. We were hopelessly overloaded: tents, stoves, sleeping-bags ... perhaps it was because Francis wanted to make sure that Luisa (whom he rather liked) did not have to rough it too much.

Mobbed by swarms of Indian children, we had passed through a whole string of little riverside villages. It had been hot, and heavy going: but now as the air grew cool and thin, and the villages more scarce, cares lifted from our shoulders, and a pleasant weariness began to descend. Where should we camp that night?

Just before dusk we reached a rather poor Indian settlement, called (as I remember) Jajachaca. Its atmosphere was as strange as its name. Nobody came out from the mean huts to greet us, save three hideous old men, more than usually far gone on coca leaves, green remnants hanging from their teeth. They blocked our path and begged for money.

There was something threatening in the air, but we made nothing of it. 'The llamas look in better condition than their owners,' Francis chuckled. 'Probably llama-rustlers.' We gave them a few small coins, and hurried on.

Night was falling fast, so, with the village now behind us and our path clinging to the edge of a high, steep gorge, we clambered down to the banks of the river, a hundred feet below. Here there was a little patch of grass. It felt safe, enclosed. The tents were soon pitched, and supper on the boil.

In the fading light Francis thought he saw a man halt for a while on the path above us, as though looking at us, and then move off. But we were not much disconcerted.

Luisa was tired by now, but quite thrilled with camping. Francis had offered to help her with her bedroll, in that 'Happy, darling?' way they do in the movies. We had pitched her tent for her, and she retired, full of relief that this was not the ordeal she had feared.

Francis and I stayed up a little, talking. After a lively argument on the financing of London Transport, he began a story about his last trip to Haiti, when one of the legion of prostitutes in Port au Prince discovered his name from his mischievous companions. Back behind the high walls of their hotel garden he had been entertaining a French girl he had just met to cocktails on the terrace, when over the parapet of the perimeter wall appeared dozens of bony hands, then dozens of soulful black faces. 'François! François!' called half the prostitutes of Hispaniola . . .

We laughed together, taken out of ourselves and, for a moment, miles from this strange gorge; then we lapsed into silence. The sound of the river seemed to grow.

Suddenly, there was a man's voice, shouting. It seemed to come from the dark path above us – high and hysterical and in no language we could understand.

I shouted back in Spanish: 'What do you want?' The response was immediate – and enraged. A scream of what sounded like abuse poured down from above.

'Come down,' Francis called, 'and talk to us.' Like all centre politicians, his instinctive preference was for dialogue.

For myself, I asked (as one always does): 'What would Mrs Thatcher do?' The answer was clear. 'Let's go for them with our penknives,' I said to Francis.

His response, again, was in character. 'No. Better find out how many of them there are, and whether they're armed. Keep them talking.' He peered up into the night. 'We're friends!' he shouted.

A great rock whistled past my ear, narrowly missing me, and thudded into Luisa's tent. She scrambled out, terrified. There was singing now, but a strange, wild sort of singing, and we were thoroughly unnerved. 'Better sing back,' said Francis. 'Sound confident.' And he launched into a tuneless rendering of 'John Brown's Body'. We had forgotten that in the Americas this is better known as 'The Battle Hymn of the Republic'. Whether or not the melody was recognisable, it provoked a hail of rocks and stones. Luisa began to cry.

There was something nightmarish about being trapped at the bottom of a gorge, your enemy above you and invisible in the dark. We crouched behind boulders and bushes, missiles raining down from the black mountain-face in front of us. But they were haphazardly aimed, for we were as invisible to the enemy as he was to us.

All my life I have been a little afraid of the dark. But now I saw that the moon was about to rise above the rock-shoulder in whose shadow we hid.

And the darkness was our friend. To find security in darkness must be an experience as old as mankind; but for me it was new, unfamiliar – and strangely exciting. Obviously we must keep away from the moonlight.

'Quickly,' I said. 'Let's get out. Let's fan out separately so we don't make an easy target. Take off your white anorak, Luisa, and follow me. Let's dodge them, get above them – meet again up there . . .'

Luisa and I crept from bush to bush, zigzagging out of the light, up towards a stretch of path away from the shouting. Francis took a different course. We could not see him and dared not call. Reaching the path, I handed Luisa the penknife and our only torch. 'Run back to the village. Stay there or bring help. We'll try to stay within sight of the tents.' She hesitated, then ran.

All our money, travellers' cheques and passports were in those tents, now bathed in moonlight. It was silly, I thought, to run off at the first scent of danger, leaving our belongings to be ransacked. We still did not know what sort of a threat we faced. I must find out.

I was free now from worrying about Luisa. And we had the advantage of being able to size up our enemy from a position unknown to him. I began to enjoy myself. This was like a boys' adventure story! I scrambled a little above the path, then slid along the mountainside in the direction of the shouting until I reached a cockpit of huge boulders, perched just above the source of the shouting. I peered out from behind the boulders.

It was only one man! He was very short and wearing a light-coloured poncho. Standing with his back to me he was yelling and loosing off rocks in the general direction of the tents. From time to time he would sway weirdly in a sort of stationary dance, holding a stone in each hand and smashing them violently together, before hurling them at what he thought was us. He seemed to be in some sort of trance.

I could have surprised him by leaping on him from behind and above, but I was not that confident of my prowess: and Luisa had the knife. I contemplated the possibilities, chuckling: I had left unfinished in London a correspondence with Sir Edward Du Cann about my hopes of assembling an all-party civil liberties group. Now I felt rather careless of this man's civil liberties.

Abruptly, the man stopped his noise. To my dismay he loped off down the path in the direction of the village. That was where Luisa had gone. Should I follow him, or find Francis?

Francis called softly from behind a nearby bush, and we rediscovered each other. I told him what had happened; but before we could decide what to do next. Luisa returned.

She was sobbing. Even in the darkness we could see that she had been in some kind of a struggle. There was earth all over her face and clothes. She told us what had happened.

She had been locked out of every hut. The village had barred its doors, all the lights within had been extinguished and when she called, nobody answered. So she had set out on the path back to us. There she had met our enemy, coming the other way, though she had not recognised him until he was almost on her. He had grabbed her, knocked her down and dragged her along the path – for no obvious reason: she had the impression that he was drugged.

It was Luisa's religion which had saved her from whatever fate was otherwise in store. Instinctively, she remembered, she had started shouting intercessions to Jesus and the Virgin Mary. It was the cries of 'Maria' which had shaken the man and he had momentarily let go. Luisa escaped and he did not follow.

We returned to our tents. But we could not contemplate staying there now. What if he came back with reinforcements? Besides, the place just felt unsafe. So we chose the boulder-lookout I had used earlier, and started to install ourselves there. From here we would have the advantage of height over anyone who came along the path.

We had ferried Francis's and Luisa's belongings up to our new hideout, and I had returned alone to fetch my own, when I heard a whistle, and looked up at the path, now bathed in brilliant white moonlight. Six men were approaching from the direction of the village. So – he had done as we feared.

I left everything behind except money and passport and ran for cover into the undergrowth, snaking my way back up to the boulders before the men reached that section of the path. This they did, stopping directly above our campsite.

I had dived into a convenient bush, below the boulders. The men were now fifty-odd yards along the path. I could see everything and hissed a commentary to Luisa and Francis, crouching behind the biggest rock with our belongings.

'There are six of them. They've spread out along the path . . .' There was an anxious pause. 'One of them's started throwing rocks . . . they're all throwing rocks . . .'

The men started shouting and whistling towards the tents.

'They think we're still there. They've stopped. They seem to be talking. They're . . . one of them is . . .'

It was at this point that the situation turned. Up until then, it had been frightening, nasty. We had been afraid – perhaps – of being beaten up, and we were certainly fearful of being robbed. But that had been about the extent of it.

But, as I watched the men set alight to the undergrowth along the path, systematically, in a wide sweep around our tents, it was suddenly clear that we might be murdered.

For people (like us) not accustomed to facing situations which encompass the possibility of death, the dawning of that thought is an odd sensation. Flat: not frightening, not sad: depressing, not scary at all. Even at the time, you feel conscious that you are not rising, emotionally, to the occasion.

Or are you? Perhaps the art of storytelling has led us to expect the wrong thing.

Storytellers must frame events like paintings. Nothing just 'happens' out of the blue. Key figures must be introduced beforehand: clues and pointers must be laid, the stage props identified. Your audience, in short, must be looking in the right direction before anything happens. Properly framed and hung, the canvas is now ready for viewing. That is what you are to look at – not the wall or the light switch.

Cast your mind back to a television film in which the cameraman himself has not been aware of the significance of what he was photographing. A crowd scene, for instance – filmed for 'background colour' – when a sudden crush, a balustrade giving way, has made the footage 'historic'. The components of the disaster are all there, but the incident, as it has since come to be called, feels flat. Why is the action in the bottom right-hand corner of the frame? What has the ice-cream vendor in centre-frame got to do with it?

Witnesses to such evidence often use the word 'disbelief' to explain why they are not feeling what they suppose the situation requires. But it is not belief that we lack. We lack the time to sort out what it means and arrange our reactions in accordance with what we believe is proper. A good narrator can make these arrangements for us, in advance of the event; but life takes us by surprise, leaves us focusing on the wrong things and unprepared to rise emotionally to the occasion. That is why art is so much more satisfactory than life.

Compare those unwitting records with the subsequent – so triumphantly subsequent – 'documentaries', in which all that was later judged irrelevant has been conveniently removed, and the reactions which were later judged appropriate conveniently inserted.

Life is so shapeless. Stories well-told make the real thing seem a continuous disappointment and saddle each of us with a secret feeling of inadequacy. Reality never coheres. Its narrative is either incoherent or it is a lie.

Instinctively we ran, clambering under cover up the mountainside. Then we stopped, out of the moonlight, to regroup, panting for lack of oxygen. In the panic, Luisa had left her rucksack back at the boulders. 'Hide and wait,' I said, rashly. 'I'll get it.'

I clambered down, and reached our old hideout fast. The view from there was terrifying. Flames were leaping from the campsite, fires crackling up the hillside towards me. In their light I could see men running back and forth. There was whistling and shouting and a dog barking. What when they realised we had got out? Surely they would come for us?

I grabbed Luisa's things and scrambled back up the mountain, towards the others.

But where were they? All the bushes looked the same and I dared not shout ... hissed whispers brought a response from underneath a large cactus bush, and the three of us huddled down together.

What were we to do?

It was no good going back to the path. One way led to the hostile village, the other led further up the blind valley – to who knows what? We did not even know from which side our attackers came, though they had approached from the village below. And there was certainly no returning to the camp itself.

So the only way was up the mountainside. Our maps were in my rucksack – burned, perhaps, by now. But I seemed to remember that high above us there was a ridge, and behind it a valley which led back down to the railway.

What I did not remember was that the ridge was 17,000 feet high. Somehow the top only looked another few hundred feet. So we just kept climbing.

By now the altitude was affecting us badly. In places the slope could only be tackled on all fours, and, sometimes, on our stomachs. Our handholds were sharp rocks and vicious cactuses with saw-like serrations down each side of every sword-shaped leaf. Our hands were soon badly cut.

We grew shorter and shorter of breath. I was exceptionally fit at the time, being in training for the London marathon, while Luisa was the weakest. Francis was basically strong, but no athlete. So, having no rucksack to carry myself, I took both his and Luisa's. This left him with the full-time job of helping Luisa, hauling her up slopes and steadying her in the more precipitous climbs.

We were spurred on by the sound of thin, distant whistles and shouts coming up from the valley below. Once we looked back and saw the opposite side of the valley lit by a great, red, flickering glow. With horror we realised that it was the reflection of our campsite – now hidden from us in the gorge. When she saw this and heard the whistling, Luisa started to cry again: this time with an edge of hysteria.

Francis was better at comforting her. I tried, too, but was alarmed to find that my real feeling was a desire to hit her. What a stupid response! As useless, in its way, as hers. I suppressed it. Soon Luisa recovered her nerve.

Up and up we scrambled, breathless to the point of nausea. We could not know it, but we had climbed nearly 3,000 feet; and it was by now some hours since we had left our campsite.

But what was worse, there was no sign that we were nearing the top. The rocks were becoming steeper. Yet, if the shouts and whistles from the valley were more distant, it did not seem so. We were overwhelmed by the feeling – hard, now, to explain or understand – that our enemies were in hot pursuit. Every night bird's shriek sounded like a whistle close at hand. Every rock we dislodged became the clatter of assailants, scrambling up behind us.

Then, to our dismay, what appeared to be a cliff-face rose sheer before us. To left and right it was impossibly steep. Yet behind and beneath us lay the valley of bandits. Upwards was still the only way.

We caught our breath as Luisa screamed. She had

momentarily lost her footing. Quickly she regained control but the mindless rhythm of climbing was snapped, and we sank to our knees, cliffs towering above us. Nobody spoke.

Through the silence came a spine-tingling sound. Far, far below us, in the dark valley, someone was playing the Indian flute. It was a thin, clear, high song: the same strange melody, repeating and repeating. 'We know where you are,' it seemed to call. 'You cannot leave. We can wait.' Luisa started to cry again. She and Francis were exhausted.

'Stay here,' I said, 'with our stuff. Rest. I'll look for a way past this cliff.'

I was soon alone, out of sight, and climbing. With nothing to carry and no companions to depend on me, all my fear dropped away from me again – as it had while I shadowed the man in the poncho. Exhilarated and free, I climbed quickly, gaining height through the broken rocks, dogged only by the thought that it would be hard for the others to follow.

The worry grew: until I came face up to a rock wall which seemed simply impossible. I stared at it for a while, and sized up the precipices to each side. Then I tried a couple of footholds.

There was a way up. I reckoned on a good chance of doing it without falling, though a fall might have been fatal. But I knew that Luisa and Francis could never make it.

I looked at the problem from all sides, and followed each possible choice through to its range of possible outcomes. It was the last of these which proved decisive.

'Whatever should I say to Francis's mother?' I thought. That clinched it. That, in the end, was the reason I went back.

Francis and Luisa were huddled together under a rock. 'We're pretty much trapped,' I said.

There seemed to be little choice. We would try to sleep until first light, then spy out the land and consider whether and how to return.

A bitter wind had got up. We were too tired, and the mountainside was too steep, for us to search for anywhere sheltered or level. But now that we had stopped moving, the cold bit deep: so I wedged myself against a cactus, wrapped in a llama-wool blanket decorated with pictures of llamas (a souvenir) and slept. The others couldn't. As I drifted away, the distant song of that flute pierced the night again: Francis and Luisa lay there waiting for the dawn, listening for an attack. None came.

Just before dawn, they woke me. In the pale light it was clear that the next outcrop beneath us afforded the best lookout, so we clambered down the mountain. What had taken hours to climb tumbled away in a fraction of the time. It was more of a controlled fall than a descent. Once, I led the other two over the edge of a small cliff, and the three of us landed, arms and legs flailing, in some thorn-scrub at its feet. Seconds later our luggage landed on top of us, but nobody was hurt – though Francis had ripped the back of his trousers in a rather final way. Perched more than a thousand feet above our campsite, we awaited the sunrise.

Agonisingly slowly, the light crept over the white ridge of the mountains. The sky was clear, the sun orange. In its light we could see right down to the river we had left so many hours before. Our campsite was still smouldering, and all around it the hillsides were blackened. But the tents themselves did not seem to have been burned. All was still. There was no sign of the bandits: not from this distance, at any rate.

Had they fled with the dawn? Or were they hiding, waiting for us?

It is remarkable how confidence returns with daylight. Many arguments, all leading to the conclusion that we were in no real danger – arguments which were as true in the dark as they were in the light – now gathered persuasive force.

Higher up the valley we could see smoke curling from the chimneys of huts. A small boy, with a little dog running beside him, was scampering from one settlement to another, his mother calling him back. Cocks were crowing, and there was music – that same flute perhaps? – coming from somewhere. This was not a world, surely, in which people were set upon?

I agreed to go down alone to the tents for a reconnaissance. The others would follow me as far as the last descent, then wait, watching me from cover. I took the penknife!

It was difficult descending into that gorge. When I reached the campsite, ashes still fresh, I had to stop for a moment to summon the courage to search it. What if they were concealed inside one of the tents? The rushing of the river near by made it worse for it deprived me of one of the senses by which I might be alerted to movement. And if Francis were to shout a warning, would I even hear?

I tried to keep watch in all directions while searching. But throwing back the tentflaps and entering each was heart-stopping.

There was nobody there.

I had not realised that the tents were fireproofed, but they must have been, for though cinders had burned holes in the fabric they were otherwise intact. But all our belongings had gone – all, that is, that we had not taken in our flight. So we still had our money and documents and two rucksacks: but my rucksack was gone, with all it contained. I smiled at the irony of losing my heaviest possession, a textbook I was studying: *Cases on Civil Liberties*. I hope the bandits found it useful. At that moment I would gladly have razed their little huts to the ground without due process of law.

I looked up to the skyline to gesture the others down. As I did so, I caught sight of the silhouetted figure of an old woman, skirts gathered, hobbling away over the hill. The others saw her too.

Anxiously, we packed the tents. There was nothing for it but to return the way we had come. We could not avoid passing the village which had so unnerved us, and shut Luisa out. I would go through the village first, unladen, ready to spring. The others would keep some way behind me, observing.

People withdrew into their houses as I passed, but nobody challenged me, nobody acknowledged me, nobody spoke. Eyes were averted. Two snowy-white llamas, shampooed and back-combed with scarlet tassels in their ears, raised their heads and stared at me with an ill grace as I passed. I signalled to the others that all was well but they could see that and had already started to catch me up.

Before they did, an old woman, looking like one of the witches in *Macbeth*, stepped out of the shadows and hailed Francis in broken Spanish.

'How are you today?' she cackled. Francis and Luisa answered that they were tired and hungry and that the night had not been good. They thought it best to confine themselves to generalities.

'Oh dear,' she smiled. 'What a pity! Tell me, which side of the mountain did you go up? People were wondering . . .' They made no reply, and quickened their step. She did not follow, but called out after them: 'The night is over. Now you are safe. Goodbye!'

When we reached the railway I slept, very, very heavily.

Nazario was wide-eyed at this story. The characters and events were as far from his own experience as they had been, then, from mine. The place – down in the south of Peru – might as well have been the South Pole for all that he knew of it. The people there were not his people. He shook hands with me – and then again with all the others, for good measure. We drank another beer.

Out of the blue, Nazario asked Mick: 'How old was your grandfather?'

'Ninety, when he died.'

'*Ninety?* Do people live so long?'

'Often longer, in England.'

'How long?'

'A hundred, even, some of them.'

There was an incredulous pause. 'Here, many people die

young, but old people when they are about sixty, usually. That is old for us.' Another pause. 'Do you think I would live to be ninety, if I came with you to England?'

As we were preparing to leave there was a whinnying, a barking of dogs, and a clatter of hoofs outside. A horse must be approaching at speed.

Very great speed, in fact, for the next thing that happened was the appearance of the front end of the horse through the open door of our bar. It had been going too fast to stop. The animal looked – startled – at us, and reversed out, saving its rider from certain decapitation.

We could see him, now, outside. He was trying to get off the horse. When he had accomplished this, and tried to walk into the bar, it became apparent that he was too drunk to stand. The barman went out and helped him in. Nazario looked embarrassed as the newcomer ordered four bottles of beer, ignoring our presence completely. He hardly seemed aware we were there.

This was an Indian of about thirty-five, dressed not unlike a cowboy, with a wide leather hat. It seemed from what he told the others that he had just ridden up from Chiquian – in four hours! He had been drinking in Chiquian and had stopped for more alcohol in one of the villages. The last part of the journey – the precipitous part, up along the sides of the valley – had been completed almost entirely in the dark. But his horse knew the way.

He was a swashbuckling customer and cut quite a dash, even in this condition. Nazario and the barman were impressed by his achievement; but it seemed to us that his horse was the real hero. She waited, untethered, outside for him. No doubt she knew the way home well enough: the only question was whether her master would be able to get back up into the saddle.

We did not stay to find out. The long walk back to Chiquian awaited us next morning.

Passing the village school ('Our Lady of Guadalupe') in the dark on the way home, I stopped, looking back towards the hills from which we had come down. There was no moon, this time, only the Southern Cross sparkling at the horizon, and the sound of the barman trying to persuade the drunken cavalier to leave.

... Free. Rather deny the light of the sun, than deny that ...

Going down was an easier business than coming up. Nazario had some business to do in Chiquian (or so he said) and was to accompany us with a donkey. Carlos had wanted to come too but was sent back to his father in Jahuacocha.

'They like to go,' Apolonia told us, 'to see the cars.'

We left a present for her: an empty plastic bottle which had once contained mineral water in Spain. It was of simple design, but fluted down the sides, and all the family had admired it ever since we arrived. It had been noticed approvingly by every Indian who had spotted it. There must have been something in the design which struck a chord with Indian taste. The family were delighted, and carried it off, rejoicing.

We too were a cheerful party. Mick was by now pretty much recovered and John had simply got used to having diarrhoea all the time. Ian's stomach was bad, but he did not talk much about it, and nothing seemed to dent his spirits.

Led by Ian, our party was escorted out of Llamac by most of the village children. He had become the Pied Piper of Llamac. He had taught the children to blow on blades of grass in cupped hands and this had become the latest craze among them. A squealing like that of a hundred bagpipes piped us out of town.

People from the village had given Nazario letters and messages crudely written on scraps of paper to take to Chiquian, some of them for onward transmission to Huaraz by the same informal method – simply handing on to an intending passenger. One girl who could not write gave him the message verbally: it was to be passed on to someone else who would in turn pass it on, verbally, to someone going to Lima.

As we left, a little girl (her mother holding her back) strained to join the throng. She had been one of Ian's tiny followers and he had taught her a word or two: but her l's and r's were muddled.

'Glingo!' she shouted as we passed: 'Glingo, Glingo.' Then, as this seemed to have no effect on us: '*Engrish* Glingo!'

6

TRAVELS IN FULHAM
AND ARGENTINA
Tim Rice

*The author (who remained Sir Tim when knighted in 1994,
disdaining to affect his first name, Timothy, in full) sprang to
fame – along with his then partner Andrew Lloyd Webber – in
1968, at the tender age of 24, with the lyrics for* Joseph and the
Amazing Technicolor Dreamcoat, *followed by* Jesus Christ
Superstar *and* Evita, *which is about to hit our screens with
Madonna playing the eponymous heroine. In recent times, the
author seems to have been concentrating on films, for his lyrics
were well to the fore in* Aladdin *and* The Lion King. *He has
been awarded no less than two Oscars, one Golden Globe, two
Tony Awards, ten Ivor Novello Awards and ten Grammy
Awards, with gold and platinum recordings of his lyrics being
accorded in twenty countries. He is probably proudest, though, of
being a splendid President of the Lord's Taverners from 1988 to
1990, such is his love of cricket, whilst his generous nature
extends to being the Honorary Chairman of the Foundation for
Sport and the Arts. In this story, the author tells of the genesis of*
Evita. *Would that inspiration came so fortuitously to all.*

One of the most fortunate journeys I have ever made
was a trip driving around the streets of Chelsea
and Fulham in search of a dinner party in 1973.
With no *A–Z* and in the pre-carphone era I became

hopelessly lost, taking twenty minutes longer to find my destination than I should have. As a result I heard the beginning of a radio programme about a remarkable woman which an efficient navigator would have missed entirely. It fired me with the desire to learn more about the lady, and the more I discovered in the following weeks the more I realised that here was a story that would make a marvellous musical.

Evita, Eva Perón, the most important female political figure Latin America has ever produced, made a fantastic journey from poverty and illegitimacy to the side of the Argentine president and to near-sainthood in just thirty-three years.

She was born Maria Eva Duarte on 17 May 1919 in Los Toldos, a village 150 miles west of Buenos Aires. Her father, Juan Duarte, never legally formalised his relationship with her mother, Juana Ibarguen, but did not allow the fact that he was married to another woman to interfere with his creation of a large family with Juana. The 'unofficial' Duarte family, of whom Eva was the youngest, did not always have an easy time.

Juan Duarte, a middle-class conservative landowner, died when Eva was only seven, and this event had a momentous effect upon his mistress and her five children. Juan's legitimate family prevented Eva's batch of Duartes from attending his funeral and their financial situation became extremely precarious. Eva never forgave the middle classes.

Eva's mother was forced to open a boarding house in Junin, an establishment that Evita's detractors have since maintained was a brothel, an unproven charge. There is no doubt, however, that the shrewd Juana missed no opportunity to use her business to improve her children's lot. Her two elder daughters eventually married two of her wealthier lodgers, and when she realised that Eva was obsessed with the theatrical world, she gave her every encouragement in her attempts to get to the big city, where dreams of becoming a star had a chance of coming true.

Agustín Magaldi, a popular tango singer of the time, came to Junin in 1934 and the fifteen-year-old Eva quickly latched on to this famous entertainer from the glittering city of Buenos Aires. Somehow Magaldi found himself returning to the capital with Eva in tow, and before long found that she had moved on to even more exciting companions.

Slowly Eva began to get small parts in theatrical productions and her photographs into magazines. She was an attractive girl, but not phenomenally so. However, right from the start, she displayed her talent for making the most of what she had. She was naturally dark and not blessed with a stunning figure. She dyed her hair blond and even when her opportunities for splashing out on fine clothes were limited, always managed to include some item of originality in her dress which normally won her a second glance from potential admirers or employers. Her greatest asset was her face, and with blond hair, her dark eyes and full sensuous lips she could appear striking indeed.

She won her first acting role of any significance in a radio play in 1939. By 1941 she was a regular star in radio dramas sponsored by a soap company and in 1943 performed in a series of dramatic broadcasts for Radio Belgrano telling the stories of famous women of the past, including Queen Elizabeth, Catherine the Great, Napoleon's Josephine and Nelson's Lady Hamilton. Around the same time she began to make a little headway in films. Her income was more than satisfactory, her escorts, now political and military as well as show business, more so. She had travelled quite a way since the rejection at her father's funeral.

But she was to go a lot further yet! Eva had done everything she could have hoped for when she left Junin in 1935, but the achievement of her earliest ambitions did not satisfy her – rather it fired her with the desire for more attention, more money, more fame, and for power.

As so often during the twentieth century, the Argentine political situation in the early 1940s was in turmoil. Among the military heavies jostling for political control was

Colonel Juan Perón, a widower of 47 when a military coup overthrew the civilian government of President Castillo in June 1943. The fateful moment when Eva Duarte and Juan Perón first met cannot be positively identified but the most likely date is 22 January 1944 at a concert held at the Luna Park Stadium in Buenos Aires to raise money for the victims of an earthquake that had recently devastated the town of San Juan. It was a truly shattering disaster – 3,500 killed and 10,000 injured – and if it was indeed the event that introduced the two most ambitious people in Argentina to each other, its tremors are still being felt today.

Eva attended the concert with a military friend, but by the end of the evening he had joined the long list of Eva Duarte's former lovers. Perón used the San Juan tragedy to his best advantage, setting up a Relief Fund via his new Ministry of Labour and Welfare, boosting his reputation as one who cared about the disadvantaged and the working classes. Eva saw in Perón a future leader of the country and thus the passport to the fulfilment of her wild aspirations. She flattered him, and encouraged his belief that he was to be the next president. Once Perón became aware of what Eva could do for him, it was inevitable that their liaison would last.

The combination of glamour and power was an extraordinary success. On 17 October 1945, after a complex sequence of coups, countercoups, plots, machinations, workers' uprisings and a little bit of luck, Juan Perón was inaugurated as President of Argentina, with his wife Eva Duarte de Perón at his side. The first phase of Eva's remarkable journey from back-street girl to high-flying, adored heroine of Argentina was over. She had been a vital factor in Perón's climb to the top of the greasy pole and only her death from cancer seven years later would remove her from her hard-won position as her nation's First Lady. Ironically, that same fact of death ensured that in the hearts and minds of many Argentines she would remain there for ever.

Eva Perón, in death as in life, has as many detractors as

admirers and, having written *Evita* the musical, Andrew Lloyd Webber and I have been attacked by both sides, which indicates that we must have done something right. But it is Eva's incredible driving ambition which remains for me her most impressive characteristic – her journey, whether fuelled by self-interest or desire to help others, by love for her kind or hatred for those not of her class, or by all these things, is one of the most fascinating I have ever encountered. I am glad my appalling sense of direction during a much shorter trip enabled me to discover this.

7

GOAT HURLING
BY MOONLIGHT
Ralph Steadman

The author, a famous freelance cartoonist, illustrator and writer, is a man of such principle that he once made a positive political statement by refusing ever again to draw another politician. He hasn't. Luckily his abstinence does not extend to other subjects and we are treated to the delights of one of his inimitable drawings. As for the story itself – is it true or false? We shall never know. What we do know is that it illustrates to perfection the author's macabre, mordant wit – which his cartoons always display with such consummate ease.

It doesn't seem to make any sense, but that's myths for you. One moment you are walking along minding your own business, then, wombbingdog!! something hits you in the face like a paralysed goat, and sure enough, it *is* a paralysed goat, and it *has* hit you in the face.

No one can explain to me this strange practice, this eerie ritual.

In Northern Chile on the road to the Atacama Desert, the driest place on earth, and location of the dreaded Valley of the Moon, where every footfall echoes around the rocky wastes like a crunchy whiplash in an empty bottle, there is a ghost town by the name of Ofcina Puelma. It was once a thriving nitrate mining town which flourished from the

155

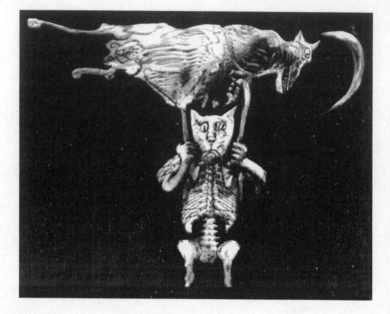

turn of the century until the Wall Street Crash of 1929, when people hurled themselves from the twenty-ninth floors and skyscraped to their deaths away from merciless ruin into unrequited overdraft oblivion. Meanwhile the Germans had found a nitrate substitute, but that does not concern us here.

The town of Ofcina Puelma sits straddled like the rotten teeth of gods on barren brown gums, empty dwellings and empty bath houses dried hollow in the midday sun and as weird and wasted as a hermit's discarded coat. A cat would crawl out of a doorway and run for cover in some other hole as the odd curious stranger passed by. At night, and especially on a night lit only by a twisted crescent moon, strange figures congregate wearing cat masks and leading puzzled goats on snake-leather thongs. Reaching the highest building in the town, the old Town Hall, broken down into uneven steps like a giddy pyramid, each in turn would clamber up to the Palladian tip of the Town Hall's façade. Uttering a puzzled cry, each would hurl their goat out into the blackness and onto the barren sandy earth below.

Most times each goat would stagger to its feet looking dazed, and occasionally one would limp away, and only rarely did one fail to rise. When one did not rise, the gathered assembly would fall to their knees, releasing the other goats to fend for themselves, whilst the assembled throng wailed through the night until the dawn cast its rational glow across the landscape, whereupon they would scamper off like embarrassed partygoers caught out by the milkman. They would jump aboard dilapidated farm trucks and born-again charabancs and head off towards the oasis town of Calama or back to Antofagasta and to their jobs in insurance and Bernardo O'Higgins banks, as they are called in the region. The only evidence that they were at Ofcina Puelma at all is the goat, stretched out and stiffening in the morning sun.

Since there are only ever desert conditions in the region, the ritual is believed to be a symbolic demonstration of the utter futility of life, the goat a biblical creature, a religious icon, half devil, half god, and the cat masks the detached self-defence mechanism employed to hide from the awful truth of it all.

PART 3

A VOYAGE TO THE SOUTHERN HEMISPHERE

1

IN THE EVENT OF AN EMERGENCY A MEMBER OF THE CREW WILL DROP DOWN IN FRONT OF YOU

John Chapman

The author, an actor-playwright, was born reluctantly in North-west London. The reluctance, the author hastens to add, relates to his birth, not the location – Shalimar Gardens, Acton – than which, to date, earth has not anything to show more fair. Having acquired his schooling in a variety of academies, he graduated to the Royal one, dedicated to Dramatic Art. Thence to acting in farce at the Whitehall Theatre and subsequently to writing it – his first farce being Dry Rot *and his second* Simple Spymen *– thus keeping the Editor in gainful employment for no less than 2,879 performances in the West End. Over the intervening years the author has strayed into television and lately into* Fresh and French Fields. *He has travelled the world seeing productions of his plays, and in the following account he visits the Antipodes where he finds the natives friendly. Thence to Bali, an island of magical beauty, and finally to Singapore where events take an unexpected turn.*

If Derek Nimmo is starring in one of your plays for a year in the West End it gives you a sense of well-being. The bank manager bows you into his office and says, 'Don't call me Mr West, just call me Nat.' You can smile broadly at the tradespeople and tip the paperboy at Christmas. As it happens, I've never actually achieved those

dizzy heights. But I came close to it once when Mr Nimmo was starring in a play of mine in Australia for a few weeks. The paperboy got his reward over the festive season, the tradespeople were able to admire my caps and bridgework, but the bank manager said don't call me at all. I said Derek was in a play of mine, but that's not strictly true. In fact it was a collaboration between me and my friend Anthony Marriott. Now there's a man who knows more about dizzy heights than Sherpa Tensing. He wrote *No Sex Please We're British*. Anthony Marriott that is, not Sherpa Tensing. I don't think Tensing ever wrote anything, except perhaps his name in the snow. Incidentally Marriott wrote *No Sex Please We're British* with the late Alistair Foot. I only wish he'd written it with me instead, because the play we wrote together, *Shut Your Eyes and Think of England*, never exactly became a household name. It had a modest success – a little too modest for my liking – but it's been translated into many languages and crops up in several countries across the globe, including Australia, where, as I say, Derek Nimmo appeared in it, with his usual insouciant charm.

Just before it opened he phoned me one day whilst he was camel-trekking across the Nullabor Plain and suggested that as my wife, Betty, had never been to Australia it would be an ideal opportunity to go over there and mix a little pleasure with business.

'Fine,' I said, 'how do we get there?' 'Well,' he said, 'the pilots are awfully reliable these days, they'll have a rough idea of the route.'

'No, what I meant was do we fly direct or break the journey and drop down en route in some exotic spot like Singapore?'

'Best to fly straight to Melbourne,' he replied, 'in case we get bad notices and the play's off by the time you get here.'

He's a card.

I'd no sooner put the phone down when I found Betty surrounded by two suitcases and a cabin trunk. She looked pensive. 'What's the problem?' I asked.

'I can't decide which case,' she said.

'Which one to take?'

'No, which one to pack first.'

Taking Derek's advice, we decided to do the outward flight in one hop and dawdle on the return trip via Bali and Singapore. The journey out was extremely long but uneventful, apart from buckling a trolley at Heathrow and crippling two porters in Melbourne. We arrived in time for the opening, which went splendidly, and then spent a week or two being wined, dined and feted.

We then flew up to Sydney to appear on a TV chat show, and then, bidding a fond farewell to Australia and watching it sink slowly in the East, we headed for a few sybaritic days in Bali. I'm not sure if they've finished building the airport there yet, but in those days it consisted of a bungalow and a winding rutted track, and that was just the runway. Our taxi to the hotel at night went the pretty way, through the undergrowth. I asked the driver if he had a compass. He laughed. 'No,' he said, 'I just use a machete.'

I have absolutely no quarrel to find with Bali, or the Balinese. It's total paradise, with beaches to die for. Bathing in the sea, however, is another matter. I would advise a stout pair of walking shoes, because you can hike to the horizon without getting your ankles wet. If we'd taken a packed lunch we could have walked to Singapore.

Which brings me to the nub of this journey, our flight home.

We were due to leave Singapore around 10.00 a.m. and we had spent two days in a five-star palace indulging ourselves on Far Eastern delights. We decided to round it all off with a delicious breakfast in a dining room that would have made the banqueting hall of Valhalla look like a Little Chef. As we sat munching our mango, Betty suddenly realised she'd left her watch in the bedroom. We dived into the lift, shot up sixty-three floors, but we were too late.

Not only her watch but all her jewellery had vanished. The management were deeply apologetic. They were at a loss to explain it. It had never happened before and it would certainly never happen again. 'Not to us,' I replied. 'They've cleaned us out.' They were at pains to know if there was anything they could do to soften the blow. 'How about reducing our bill?' I said. When Orientals laugh they put their heart and soul into it. The counter was awash with tears of innocent merriment. Their shoulders were still shaking when they waved us off to the airport.

We took off at 10.00 a.m. At 10.20 Betty asked me how far we'd travelled. I'm not a whizz at mental arithmetic but with the aid of a pen and the back of two menus and a sickbag I worked out that if a plane goes at roughly 500 miles an hour after twenty minutes it will have travelled 166 miles, give or take a mile. 'There's your answer,' I said. '166 miles.'

'But it's now 10.30. How many more miles is that?'

She knows how to take the boredom out of a long flight. I returned to my labours and gave her an update. 'Two hundred and forty miles, which puts us somewhere over the Strait of Malacca.'

'Do they have control towers in the Strait of Malacca?' she enquired.

'Highly unlikely,' I said. 'Could be a hazard to shipping.'

'Well, all I've seen out of this window since we took off is that control tower.' She pointed to it. 'We're going round in circles. Why?'

'I've no idea,' I hedged. 'Ask me some more arithmetic.'

At that moment a voice from the cockpit announced that there was a minor technical problem and the plane was gradually dumping its fuel. 'What's a minor technical problem?' asked Betty. She can be a right little chatterbox at times.

'Well, it means it's not a major one, like a wing falling off, or they'd forgotten to put the duty-free on board.'

A member of the crew came running up the aisle and stopped at my seat. He had a box of tools in his hand. 'Excuse me, sir, would you mind holding this?'

'Not a bit.'

'And lift your feet sir, I've got to take the carpet up.'

'Couldn't it wait till we get to London,' I said. 'I mean, it's hardly worn.'

Give him his due, he smiled.

'No, sir, I have to remove the carpet in order to take up a floorboard.'

When you've done two years at RADA, three years in weekly rep, and co-starred in the West End, it gives you that extra confidence in public speaking. Added to which I'd seen Dame Edith Evans in *The Importance of Being Earnest*, so I gave it my best shot. 'A floor bo-o-o–ard?'

There was a slight ripple of applause from the nearby seats.

'Yes, sir,' said the mechanic. 'If I take it up I can have a look at what's underneath.'

I could see the logic of this, and two minutes later I could see the sea. 'I believe you mentioned something about a minor problem,' I said.

'Yes, sir, it's the undercarriage, it's stuck,' he replied. 'Would you be so good as to pass me a spanner?'

RADA provide excellent classes in deportment, diction and fencing but it is woefully short on engineering. I was outwardly calm, but my mind was racing. I started to fumble through the box.

'It's a wrench,' he said, with some agitation.

'Oh, it must be,' I said. 'The thought of losing a plane that's become part of your life, like a wife or a mistress, must be awful. I expect there's a strong feeling of camarad-erie on the flight deck at this moment.'

I could tell he was under some strain, the way his eyes bulged. I returned to the tool box. 'Now, what was it you, er . . .' Betty pointed to a long metal object with a sort of round lump at one end.

'Ah, bingo! Spanner!' I proffered it to him. He grabbed it and beavered away through the hole in the floor. I made a mental note never to travel in future without a spanner, or a wife. Presently the man's arm shot up.

'Screwdriver!' he shouted. I retrieved the spanner and

put the screwdriver into his hand. His top half disappeared again. I turned to see how Betty was faring. Her hair was flying every which way in a force ten gale. 'It won't be long now,' I said, trying to sound reassuring.

'No, I don't think it will,' she replied.

The mechanic's arm shot up again. 'Hammer.'

I was well into the routine by now and the transfer was effected with surgical precision. It was a good hammer as hammers go, and as hammers go it went. 'Bother!' said the mechanic, at least I think it was 'bother' but with the noise from the wind and the engines, coming up through the hole in the fuselage, it was difficult to tell. I was frantically searching for the forceps when he started to replace the floorboard.

'Well, it was worth a try,' he said.

'What's the prognosis?' I enquired.

'Difficult to say. The undercarriage is definitely down. But we don't know if it is stuck down or hanging down. If it is stuck down, locked into position, then there's no problem in landing. But if it's just hanging loose ... well ...' His voice trailed off.

'You mean, we may hear a sort of scraping sound?'

He nodded. 'Thanks for your help.'

'Anytime,' I said. 'You know where to find me. Row 12. Aisle seat.'

Ten minutes later a voice over the tannoy advised us to take up our positions for an emergency landing. We leant forward, shut our eyes and thought of England.

Fifteen minutes later, we were safely back in the airport.

We bought a lady's wristwatch and several brandies. After sixteen years Betty still has the watch, and the odd brandy.

2

IT RUNS IN THE FAMILY
Ray Cooney

The author, an actor-playwright, but a producer, director and theatre-owner as well, was – like John Chapman – an actor at the Whitehall Theatre. He, too, graduated to writing farces for the Editor – One for the Pot and Chase Me Comrade! – and has continued with his arcane craft ever since, sometimes with John Chapman, sometimes with others, but generally on his own and generally with a box-office hit on his hands. In this further antipodean airline story the author (who is renowned for his double entendres and confusion) describes a flight to the land of Oz which was as full of double entendres and confusion as any of his comedies – but the joke was on him.

As the Reader is probably aware, one of the better-known travel companies in the world is Kuoni. However, in the early 1980s, Kuoni had not yet reached its present status in this ever-increasing market.

In 1983 my comedy, *Run for Your Wife!*, had opened very successfully in London and my wife, Linda, and I were flying Qantas to Sydney where I was to direct the Australian production. Having spent nearly twenty hours in the air (with a couple of touch-downs) we were nearing the end of the flight and approaching Sydney when one of the Australian stewardesses walked along the aisle and asked

169

for our attention – which we all duly gave her. 'Are there any Cooneys on board?' she enquired. I immediately put my hand up. 'How many?' she asked. 'Two,' I replied. 'My wife and myself.'

I assumed that there was a message for us. Probably the theatrical producers who were presenting *Run for Your Wife!* in Australia had arranged for a car to meet us. However, instead of giving us a message the stewardess scribbled something on her notepad. She then looked up. 'Are there any more Cooneys?' she asked. Linda and I exchanged a glance. Before we could comment to each other on what appeared to be a strange question, a passenger further down the plane put his hand up. 'How many?' asked the stewardess. 'Two,' came the reply.

Now, I was pretty surprised. 'Cooney' is rather an unusual name. Well, maybe not in Dublin or Belfast, but outside of Ireland and New York I've rarely come across another Cooney, and why would the airline be enquiring after more Cooneys? I turned to Linda and said, 'What the devil do you think's going on?' She could only shrug her shoulders.

However, by now more hands were shooting up from amongst our fellow passengers. 'Three Cooneys here, Miss.' 'Two adult Cooneys and two children.' 'One Cooney.' 'Four Cooneys.'

My eyes were getting wider and wider. I couldn't believe it. All these Cooneys! And all on this flight! I turned to one of the other Cooneys. 'Are you a Cooney?' I asked incredulously. He nodded. He didn't look amazed. He didn't even look surprised. In fact he seemed rather nonplussed at my enthusiasm for discovering so many Cooneys on board.

It may have been the lack of sleep. It may have been the never-ending supply of alcoholic beverages during the long flight. In any event I should have realised. But neither I nor Linda had heard of the travel firm Kuoni – so how could we know that, as pronounced by the Australian stewardess, it was 'Cooney'.

Still, the stewardess pressed on down the aisle of the

plane. 'Any more Cooneys?' she demanded. More hands went up. She made notes on her pad.

Then I realised! This was obviously some wonderful publicity stunt dreamt up by the Australian producers of *Run for Your Wife!* Somehow or other they had unearthed a bunch of Cooneys, flown them over especially, and there'd be television cameras at Sydney airport to cover the arrival of the Cooney clan – a sort of 'Ray Cooney – This is Your Life'.

By now we were coming in to land and Linda and I were conjecturing on how exactly this wonderful publicity gimmick would unfold. I was more than somewhat surprised that not one of the other Cooneys seemed as excited as I was at this 'family gathering', but I put this down to the fact that they must have been sworn to secrecy to maintain the element of surprise for me.

Prior to disembarking, the stewardess once again requested our attention. 'Would all the Cooneys kindly give me their attention.' I smiled happily at my 'relations'. 'As you know, all you Cooneys are travelling on to Melbourne. On disembarking you must follow the signs which say "Transit Lounge".'

I put my hand up. 'Do you have a problem, sir?' she enquired.

'Yes, I do,' I said, 'I'm not going to Melbourne, I'm staying here in Sydney.'

'No,' she said sweetly as though talking to an idiot. 'You're going to Melbourne.'

I was in the process of explaining that I had work to do in Sydney and that, as lovely as Melbourne undoubtedly was, I needed to remain in Sydney when she suddenly interrupted me. 'Are you a Cooney?' she said sternly.

'Yes,' I replied.

'Then you are going to Melbourne with all the other Cooneys!'

I failed to see the logic of this. 'Why don't you show the young lady your ticket,' my wife suggested. I produced our tickets.

The stewardess, without opening the ticket, looked at the

cover and said tersely, 'You're *not* a Cooney!' For a moment my mind whirled. It had been a long flight. Jet-lag does funny things. 'If you look inside, I think you'll find my name . . .'

She interrupted me. 'I don't have to look inside, sir! This is not a Cooney ticket!' By now we had everybody's attention and I was getting decidedly embarrassed.

I grabbed the ticket back and opened it for her, jabbing my finger at my name. She looked. Then, after a moment she burst into laughter. 'Your name's Cooney!' she spluttered. I looked at Linda blankly. 'Hey!' said the stewardess to obtain the attention of the dozen or so other Cooneys. 'This fellow's *name* is Cooney!' My fellow Cooneys seemed to find this as amusing as the stewardess.

I was now becoming quite scared. I'm usually very good at seeing the funny side of things. I asked Linda if I was missing the point of something but by now she'd buried herself in her in-flight magazine, having decided to leave me to face the madness of the stewardess alone.

The stewardess handed me back the tickets, her mascara running down her face from the laughter. 'That's great!' she said. 'Here's me thinking you're a "Cooney" – and you're a *Cooney*.' By now the whole plane was dissolved into laughter. Linda continued to study her in-flight magazine. I attempted to offer up a polite smile.

Whilst disembarking I tried to ignore the giggles from the entire crew, who had obviously had me pointed out to them. And the walk to the Baggage Claim seemed an eternity as my fellow 'Cooney' passengers on their way to the transit lounge waved farewell with unrestrained laughter. It was only then that Linda pointed out to me that each was carrying a similar carry-on bag emblazoned boldly with the name Kuoni. The penny finally dropped!

Having eventually got through Customs, we were spilling out into the main hall when a gentleman in a peaked cap approached us and asked, 'Are you Cooneys?'

'*No!*' I replied hastily and whisked my wife away to the queue at the taxi rank.

I arrived at the theatre to be greeted by an apologetic producer. 'How on earth did our driver miss you?' he asked. I might have known – the gentleman in the peaked cap wasn't the Kuoni representative.

I suppose I should be grateful I wasn't born Thomas Cook.

3

A HAND OF CARDS
Michael Frayn

The author, renowned as a columnist, a playwright, a scriptwriter and a peerless adapter of the works of Chekhov, is probably best known to the theatre-going public as the dramatist responsible for Noises Off, *which won the 1982* Evening Standard *Award for Best Comedy and also the (now entitled) Olivier Award in the same category. These trophies added to many more which have come his way and now adorn his mantelpiece. In this little tale, the author keeps us up to date with family news from New Zealand.*

Bernard –

> *With All Good Wishes*
> *for a Merry Christmas*
> *and a Happy New Year!*
>   – from Charles (Edwards!)

    I don't know whether you remember me – we used to prop up the bar of the Rose and Crown together occasionally in the good old days, in dear old London town. How are you keeping back there in England, you old reprobate? Look me up if you're ever passing through New Zealand.

*

Bernard and Jean –

> *Wishing You a Very*
> *Merry Christmas and the*
> *Happiest of New Years*
> > – from Charles

Congratulations on your marriage – saw it in the *Times* airmail edition. Nice work if you can get it. Meant to write on the spot. Anyway, cheers to you both.

*

Bernard, Jean, and Baby Flora(!) –

> *All Best Wishes for*
> *Xmas and the New Year*
> > – from Charles and Kitty(!)

Charles took the plunge at last, as you can see! Many congrats on the Flora effort – saw it in *The Times* – meant to write. You must come out and see us some time.

*

Bernard, Jean, Flora, and Polly(!) –

> *To Wish You a*
> *Joyous Christmas*
> > – from Charles, Kitty, Gareth(!),
> > and Luke(!!)

Yes, you did hear right – twins! Identical – fair, with Charles's nose and mouth. Born 14 July – same day as Fall of Bastille! Charles had to be revived with brandy. Gareth ate ear-ring last month, otherwise everything OK. Tremendous congrats on Polly – meant to write.

*

Jean, Flora and Polly –

> *The mail coach dashes thru' the snowy ways.*
> *To bring good cheer and news of happy days!*
> > – from Charles, Kitty, Gareth,
> > Luke, Lionel(!), and Mother.

Dreadfully sorry about you and Bernard, but I'm sure you're usually better off apart in these cases. Great shock when we got your last year's card, meant to write at once, but you know how it is, particularly with Lionel and all the rest of it. Lionel was a slight mistake, of course! Mother's moved in to help out.

*

Bernard, Jean, Flora, Polly, and Daisy(!) –

> *Peace on Earth, Goodwill to Men*
> – from Kitty and Walter
> (CRAIGIE!), not to mention
> Gareth, Luke, Lionel, Mother,
> Victoria and Georgina!

Heartiest congrats on you and Bernard getting together again – further hearty congrats on weighing in so smartly with Daisy! Meant to write as soon as your last Xmas card arrived. Walter and I were married in Auckland on 9 June, reception for 120, two days' honeymoon at Rotorua while mother looked after children. Victoria and Georgina are Walter's children by first marriage, of course(!) Walter is engineer – low temperature. Poor Charles is coming over to England in New Year, told him to look you up.

*

Bernard, Jean, Flora, Polly, Daisy, and James(!) –

> *Hearty Good Wishes for*
> *a Merry Xmas and a*
> *Prosperous New Year!*
> – from Kitty, Walter, Gareth,
> Luke, Lionel, Mother, Victoria,
> Georgina, Murray, Lester and
> Baby Linda.

Congrats on James – my word you keep at it! Victoria and Georgina had lovely joint wedding at St Margaret's, Wanganui, in Feb. Vicky married Murray West (his father's in agricultural machinery down near Christchurch),

Georgie married Lester Dewie – nice young man, went to school in England (Thorpehurst – know it?), now learning hotel business. Georgie's baby Linda born (prematurely!) 3 Aug. Did poor Charles ever show up in GB?

*

Charles(!), Jean, Flora, Polly, Daisy, and James –

> *When the Yule log brightly burns*
> *And brings its Christmas cheer,*
> *To days gone by fond Mem'ry turns,*
> *And old friends far and near!*
> > – from Kitty, Walter, Gareth,
> > Luke, Lionel, Victoria, Murray,
> > Georgina, Lester, Linda, Sukie,
> > and Simon.

Heartiest congrats from all of us on you and Charles! V. best wishes – all tickled pink. Shameful of me not to write in summer when I heard news but Vicky was just producing Simon, and then Georgie was having Sukie while I looked after Linda, then Mother passed quietly away.

*

Charles, Jean, Flora, Polly, Daisy, James, Dinah(!), Gareth, Luke, and Lionel –

> *Yuletide Greetings!*
> > – from Kitty, Walter, Victoria,
> > Murray, Georgina, Lester, Linda,
> > Sukie, Simon, and Gabriel.

Congratulations on Dinah! Don't know how you do it! Gabriel (Simon's brother) born 7 Oct. in flood. Hope Gareth, Luke, and Lionel are settling down all right with their father for Xmas, seems very quiet here without them, though Lester's mother is coming for Xmas Day (she's just lost her husband, sadly) plus his two sisters Charmian and Henrietta, so house will be quite full. Walter has ulcer.

*

178

Charles, Jean, Flora, Polly, Daisy, James, Dinah, Gareth, Luke, Lionel, Georgina, Lester, Linda, Sukie, and Jane –

> *Christmas Comes But Once a Year,*
> *and When it Comes it Brings Good Cheer!*
>> – from Kitty, Walter, Victoria,
>> Murray, Simon, Gabriel,
>> Nicholas, Charmian, Henrietta,
>> *Bernard*(!), Cecilia, and Timothy.

Hope the boys are enjoying their Xmas jaunt as usual and behaving themselves. So good of you to have Georgie and Lester and the girls for Xmas while they're over in England, hope Charles will be up and about again soon. Guess what, Bernard's here! Coming for Xmas Day with his new wife Cecilia and their baby Timothy (three months). Sends his love – says he doesn't send Xmas cards any more. I know what he means – once you start it never ends.

4

TUSITALA: ROBERT LOUIS STEVENSON IN THE SOUTH SEAS

Leslie Thomas

The author, one of the most celebrated of the current crop of successful old boys whose alma mater was Dr Barnardo's, began his writing career as a reporter for local newspapers in the London area and then graduated to the London Evening News. *His first novel,* The Virgin Soldiers, *published in 1966, was an instant best-seller and he has produced equally successful books almost every year since then. Like the Publisher, the Editor, the Illustrator and divers other writers, he is an ardent cricket supporter and keeps his eye firmly on the ball with this delightful little innings (first reported in* The Times*), exploring the last years of a fellow great novelist, Robert Louis Stevenson.*

From Bournemouth to the South Seas had been a long and wandering journey, and Robert Louis Stevenson and his wife were grateful when, in September 1890, they reached Samoa for this was to be their home for the rest of their lives together. The quest for wealth and contentment was done. It was a brief triumph but by then, only to be expected.

They had bought land on the island of Upolu, the most central and important in the group of Samoa; four hundred acres, three miles from Apia, the capital, on a shelf of a tropic hill overlooking the Pacific Ocean. The house they

were to build there already had a name – Vailima – in the Samoan language, Five Waters, for white streams ran down the slope like the fingers of one hand.

Fanny Stevenson, in her diary of a century ago, forgot to enter the date. 'Arrived at Vailima on the ... day of September ... A very neat and expensive building, very like a bandstand in a German beer garden, has been built in the corner above the small waterfall.'

In the past three years they had travelled from England to New York State, to California, where they had once honeymooned in a shack by a silver mine, and then on to Honolulu and the isles of the Pacific. They moved *en famille* and in some style for Robert Louis Stevenson at thirty-seven had written *Treasure Island*, *Kidnapped* and, more importantly, *Dr Jekyll and Mr Hyde*. His mother and, inter-mittently, Fanny's son Lloyd and her daughter Belle trav-elled with them. The object of the peripatetic journey was health and exploration, especially health.

Most of us can misquote the epitaph which Stevenson composed for his grave in Samoa, and which correctly reads:

> Home is the sailor, home from sea
> And the hunter home from the hill.

How he reached that remote island hilltop is not so well appreciated. He had selected Samoa as his final exile for the very good reason that it was on the shipping route between Australia and the West Coast of the United States, and thus overland and transatlantic to Britain; he could not only get his manuscripts *out* but he could get his royalties *in*.

He had tried the enchantments of Tahiti but the com-munications were not so good. He was ever a businesslike writer.

It was in the village of Taurita on Tahiti that I first became aware of the tropical trail left over those years by the Stevenson family. There they were entertained by the chief, given a royal house, and Robert Louis Stevenson strolled around in pyjamas. His mother, strong and religious, left the gift of a silver Communion service that is still in use in the native church today.

I discovered that in the Marquesas Islands, where Paul Gauguin is buried (he missed Stevenson in Tahiti by one year) the family had lived with native chiefs who both drank and dressed excessively. American and Australian traders had left them with an abundance of exotic and, in the main, useless possessions. It was not unusual to see a chief, much the worse for wear, adorned in a top hat and red flannel drawers, and carrying a sewing machine. They had so many sewing machines (in a society where clothes were minimal) that they used them as anchors for their boats. The Stevensons went enjoyably native. 'I wish you could but just get a glimpse of that lady taking a moonlight promenade on the beach in the company of a gentleman dressed in a single handkerchief,' Fanny wrote to Henry James of her mother-in-law.

In Honolulu this year, staying two blocks back from the tourist strip of Waikiki, I was drawn by a strangely compelling painting (in the hotel coffee shop!). It was painted in 1969 by Bernard de Veas but, although depicting a scene eighty years before, it had a marvellous sense of truth. It shows the Stevenson family being entertained to a dinner-cum-picnic by King Kalakaua of Hawaii, a lively if some what odd monarch who conducted his own band, put tramcars on the streets of Honolulu, and built an opera house with electric light. In the foreground of the picture squats Robert Louis Stevenson, a figure so modern and demanding attention that it is tempting to say 'nearest the camera'. He wears a light brown suit and the famous penetrating eyes pin the viewer from behind rimless spectacles. He appears to be about to make a polite but incisive enquiry just before you move away.

Among the stacked surfboards, sunsoakers and swimmers in the pool of the Moana hotel, facing Waikiki Beach and at the hub of the jazzy strip, is a noble banyan tree below which the author rested and wrote during his time in Hawaii. It has grown more roots and branches in the century since and spreads majestically, shading the splashing Japanese tourists as it once shaded a famous writer.

From his tubercular childhood in Edinburgh, Robert Louis Stevenson had never been far from illness and sometimes death. His youth had been one long trek from doctor to doctor, cure to cure, spa to spa. At Bournemouth, where he had high but ultimately disappointed hopes of the curative properties of the Scots pines, he believed he could be both at home and well.

In his house called Skerrvore, named after a Scottish lighthouse designed by his engineer father (at the gate was a model lighthouse which lit at evening), Stevenson and his American divorcee wife, ten years his senior, had held modest court, and he had written *Kidnapped* and *Dr Jekyll and Mr Hyde*. The latter, despite the success of *Treasure Island*, was the book which brought him universal fame. It was read by people who had never paid a shilling for a book before, and it was used as a text for sermons. But fame and fortune were not matched by the thing he required most. 'I do not ask for health,' he said. 'But I will go anywhere and live in any place where I can enjoy the ordinary existence of a human being.' Bournemouth had failed him.

On a flotilla of ships, liners, freighters (one with a cargo of apes) and chartered yachts, he and Fanny and interchanging relatives and servants roamed the seas to find his healthful haven. In Honolulu he shrank from the chill of the Trade Winds, from Sydney he retreated coughing. 'It is more the capital of the New South Pole than New South Wales.'

He and Fanny, often eccentric and moody, but strong for him, were wary of taking any place on first impressions. There had been too many disappointments. In the South of France they had dubbed Hyères the perfect spot, only to be driven away by cholera. They had also begun to realise that the curse of so-called health resorts was that they were full of sick people. They needed somewhere without clinics and wheelchairs; without doctors and diets; a place where not so many people were dying.

Stevenson was happy at sea and the South Seas brought him respite from the wracking of consumption. It had been declared arrested by a specialist in the United States, but the dreaded haemorrhaging struck him on too many occasions to bring him to believe the diagnosis. Once sailing below the blue of Capricorn, and among the warming islands, he found an amazing and gratifying return to wholeness. He rambled, climbed, rode for hours on horseback, fished and waded into the Pacific breakers. He also smoked frequently, as did Fanny; they rolled their own.

The lives of sea-nomads had lent them an added rough and eccentric appearance. When they first arrived, with Lloyd, Fanny's son, and walked up the main street of Apia, Samoa, they were taken to be a troupe of itinerant entertainers, acrobats perhaps. But, by showing a photograph of Robert Louis Stevenson with King Kalakaua of Hawaii, which had been their social passport throughout the coral islands, they were able to establish that they were people of importance.

Apia, a dirt street with shanty buildings, must have presented as odd a sight to the Stevensons as they did to its residents. For although this was a remote harbour, in a backwater island, it was the axis of international politics in the Pacific. Britain, the United States and Germany, all had fingers in the Samoan pie. They argued and edged and manoeuvred in their Western ways while their variously favoured local chiefs went frequently to war with each other. Fanny noted in her diary a visit from a departing chief who had come to pay his respects before going off with 150 armed men 'to take possession of the women, children and old men of the Mataafa faction'.

This mere squabbling, however, was a backcloth to jostlings of the great powers. In Apia harbour, as the Stevensons landed, were five wrecked warships, German and American, thrown aside by a recent hurricane. They might have escaped its major fury if they had sailed for the open sea, but each captain was frightened of leaving the others in possession of the anchorage. The wreck of the German corvette remained visible on the rocks for sixty years.

Having decided that this physically tranquil but humanly lively place was where they wanted to live, Robert Louis and Fanny bought a shelf of land – four hundred acres at a pound an acre – and set in motion the building of a house. They then went on their voyages once more, to the islands, to Australia, and returned that September day in 1890. By this time they had realised that it was unlikely that they would ever see Europe or even America again. Robert Louis Stevenson had arrived in Samoa to live and to die.

On the serene hilltop in the South Pacific, Louis and Fanny began work on their paradise. Stevenson exalted in the physical labour, as did Fanny. Never healthier in his life, he set about clearing land, helping with the building of the house, making weatherproof the temporary shelter they inhabited in the company of servants and animals, and organising the ascent of the uncertain track from Apia. Fanny, who had made gardens in all their dwellings, rejoiced in the fruitfulness of Samoa, the way flowers grew almost overnight.

Their enthusiasm, however, failed to communicate itself to others. The American historian Henry Adams found them in 'squalor like a railroad navvy's board hut ... a man so thin and emaciated that he looked like a bundle of sticks in a bag ... dirty striped pyjamas, the baggy legs tucked into coarse woollen stockings, one of which was bright brown in colour, the other a purplish dark tone ... a woman ... the usual missionary nightgown which was no cleaner than her husband's shirt and drawers ... like a half-breed Mexican.'

Although he could not forget the dirt and discomfort (and the pointed suggestion that if he came to breakfast he should bring his own food, as supplies were short) Adams found Stevenson entertaining. 'He cannot be quiet, but sits down and jumps up, darts off and flies back, at every sentence he utters, and his eyes and features gleam with a hectic glow . . . like an insane stork.'

Even if the objects of Adams' description had known his reactions it is doubtful if they would have worried. They were literally in paradise. The author not only knew that he had found his haven but was pleased (as a man who was never averse to publicity and praise might be) when he heard from Edmund Gosse in London: 'Since Byron was in Greece, nothing has appealed to the ordinary literary man as much as that you should be living in the South Seas.'

When it was finally complete, the glory of Vailima was the great hall which occupied the whole of the ground floor of the main house. It was sixty feet by forty and roofed with Californian redwood. Two Burmese gilded gods were positioned at the foot of the magnificent central staircase.

Samoan chiefs who came visiting viewed with interest the fireplaces (they were useful for airing the Stevenson sheets), and asked politely if the Burmese gods were alive in the same manner as they enquired after the existence of a magic bottle from which the illustrious white man received all his money and power. They could not comprehend that merely writing words on paper could bring such wealth. The suspicion was reinforced when Stevenson wrote his story 'The Bottle Imp', which was translated into Samoan and published in a missionary paper. It was all they needed to convince them.

From the natives Stevenson received his celebrated name 'Tusitala', the teller of tales, although he himself whimsically translated it as 'The Great White Information Man'. Practical Fanny, known for her sleeves-rolled-up bustle, was called 'Aolele' – the flying cloud. In everyday language, however, the writer was also named Ona – literally the Owner, because of his house and all his wonderful possessions.

Mrs Thomas Stevenson had long become a permanent member of the household. Every day she would make a brief smiling bow to the bust of her late husband, buried in far off Edinburgh, which beamed genially over the great hall. Lloyd, Fanny's son, and her daughter Belle, her marriage to a layabout artist Joe Strong finished, lived also at Vailima. When writer's cramp added itself to Stevenson's ills, she became his amanuensis, taking dictation for two or three hours a day. It was no light task. In his four years in Samoa, Robert Louis Stevenson had an output of about three quarters of a million words, letters, diaries, poetry, his novel *Catriona*, and the unfinished novel *St Ives*. He also wrote recipes for native dishes. And prayers.

With the barefoot, bare-breasted servants of the house and his family assembly, he would pray: 'We thank Thee for this place in which we dwell; for the love that unites us ... for the health, the work, the food and the bright skies that make our lives delightful; for our friends in all parts of the earth and our friendly helpers in this foreign isle.'

His London literary friends, Gosse, Henry James, Sidney Colvin, he missed most of all. But there was an entertaining passage of people who visited Samoa and attended one of the great dinner and dancing nights at Vailima. There were also Europeans living in and around Apia who delighted in his hospitality and his words. Rider Haggard's brother, Bazett, was there; and to one little girl, Annie Ide, daughter of the US Land Commissioner, born on Christmas Day, he gave the celebrated gift of *his* birthday, so that she would not miss out on the presents.

So content was he with life at Vailima that Stevenson, ever of a prospecting nature, never explored the other parts of the island of Upolu. The path to the villages at the extreme of his own island, which passed his door, went untrodden by him. He liked to be home by nightfall. The family furniture had been shipped from Bournemouth and Edinburgh, he had his books, his pictures. He was completely at home.

On 3 December 1894 he lunched with Bazett Haggard, who was the British Land Commissioner. He was in bustling spirits the next morning; he dictated to Belle what were to be his final written words, for his novel *The Weir of Hermiston*. By early evening he was helping Fanny to prepare dinner, experimenting with a salad dressing, when he abruptly cried out 'Oh, what a pain!' and staggered back. 'Do I look pale?' he asked his wife. They were his last words.

He collapsed into unconsciousness and never recovered. It was a massive cerebral haemorrhage. Doctors came from the town and from a British warship. Dr Anderson, from HMS *Wallaroo*, seeing the stick-like forearms of the famous man, exclaimed: 'How can a body write books with arms like that?'

He died with his Samoan servants and friends kneeling around him, 'making a church'. The body was lying on a table which had been in his childhood home in Edinburgh. The following day he was carried to the hilltop (a path having been hurriedly cut in the night) and there he was laid as he had wanted, under the wide and starry sky. The frail, undaunted adventurer who had written 'Home is the sailor, home from sea, the hunter home from the hill' had died making mayonnaise. He was forty-four.

PART 4

A VOYAGE TO
THE INDIAN
SUBCONTINENT
AND THENCE
TO THE
WESTERING
REACHES OF
THE IBERIAN
PENINSULA

1

AN ARRANGED
MARRIAGE
Melvyn Bragg

*The author is a novelist and broadcaster of renown, with 'Start
the Week' on Radio 4 and 'The South Bank Show' on London
Weekend Television as his best-known presentations. He is also
the Controller of Arts, LWT, the Chairman of Border Television,
the President of the National Campaign for the Arts, and a
successful dramatist. In this tale of university life in India (which
first appeared in* Punch *in 1981) the author conjures up a sad
story of unrequited love.*

It began soon after I arrived at the University for a three-
month start as a visiting lecturer.

Baschia was in the English Department. He was an
elegant young Brahmin who had completed his education
in America. The quality of his published work, on the
contemporary American novel, would almost certainly
have guaranteed him a post in one of the better colleges
there. But he had insisted on returning to what he only
half-ironically called 'my native soil'. He would smile after
using the phrase, look around at the desert landscape which
provided a barren carpet for most of this impoverished
Indian province, and add: 'As you can see – soil is about all
we have to offer.' By such low-key self-mockeries he would
deflect any criticism of the place he clearly loved.

She was called Sushma and she had come to the University to do her MA on the novels of Saul Bellow. Many of the young women on the campus were lovely to look at – the sensuous composure, the rather long oval faces set off by expressions lit up with innocent merriness: Sushma was a beauty. Baschia fell for her the moment he set eyes on her.

'It's quite interesting,' he would say, striving to minimise and at the same time explain his blatant love-sickness. 'The phrase "love at first sight" – so rich in meaning to both our cultures – to all cultures quite possibly – is yet no more than a figure of speech until it happens to oneself.' Yes, Baschia, we would say, trying not to smile. He was so intoxicated that by his own countrymen's standards he was behaving most unbecomingly – though with an honourable naiveté and charming formality. 'I am sorry to bring up the subject of Sushma yet again,' he would say, when he had been out of her sight for some intolerable time – say a couple of hours – 'but Dr Mitra was saying the other day that he thought she was a little too tall not much – but just a little *too* tall. What is your opinion?' And again we would give all our attention to him because it was so nice and so rare to see such a fine man so wonderfully in love with such a beauty.

They walked together from lecture to lecture. He would chop up the pattern of his own studies and his own teaching to escort her from the English Studies building to the Canteen or the General Humanities faculty or the Hostel. He always had his umbrella – to shade her from the sun or protect her from the rain. It was just before the monsoons when the weather could alter violently.

They were lovely to watch and soon they became part of our daily conversation. 'I saw them this morning in the old town – about six o'clock. I believe he was showing her the Tantric temple: she looked very interested!' And we would nod happily at the thought and gain a little extra pleasure from the picture of him being the earnest teacher, she the solemn student. For they never touched in public, they did not hold hands; they could indeed have been mistaken by the uninitiated for teacher and student. 'I saw them in the lunch hour, in the blazing heat, over where they keep promising to build the Sports-drome – she was wearing one of those marvellous golden saris of hers: Baschia of course was looking like a peasant, as usual!' And yet again there would be complicity – for her wealthy parents endowed her with clothes fit indeed for her beauty and Baschia's principles decreed that, unlike all his colleagues, he should revert to traditional Indian peasant wear. In those few weeks, while he wooed her and won her in as courtly a way as could be imagined, they were like figures from a jewelled and precious miniature painting come to life as reminders of magic and fortune on this otherwise dull and bare plain in the middle of India.

'What will happen now?' I asked my friend Dr Mitra. 'Oh, his parents will approach her parents. They will have their horoscopes taken. The usual procedures.' Dr Mitra enjoyed guiding me through the infinite variety of Indian social codes. 'To all intents and purposes it will go ahead like all our arranged marriages. They have had the luck to fall in love and spend time getting to know each other.' That latter phrase sounded rather a tame description of the passion that clearly possessed Baschia, but I thought no more of it at the time. The extent and the apparent success of these arranged marriages still daunted me. From my English viewpoint, the system seemed to drive out all love and all liberty: yet, it worked so well; I was still, as it were, collecting evidence on that.

Unexpected and most unwelcome evidence came soon. Dr Mitra told me that Sushma had moved in with Baschia. He had the usual senior lecturer's flat on the outskirts of the campus. This 'shacking up together', so common in the West, was greeted with dismay and sadness by everyone in the University. People felt let down. More than that they truly mourned what they predicted as the end of any real chance of happiness for the young couple. And they felt that the place would suffer some slight dishonour.

Yet their behaviour was good. The jokes went and so did all the tender by-play of reference – but the couple were not ostracised nor were they publicly or privately rebuked. But people withdrew. Where before there had been a sense in which everyone was participating in this wonderful drama, there was now a distinct and rather ominous feeling of pulling back to a boundary, no longer being prepared to participate, watching the drama from the sidelines. To the observers, the outcome was very obvious.

Dr Mitra was reluctant to talk about it – the whole business upset him too much. Baschia was not only a particular friend but someone he had admired in a whole-hearted and loving way. Eventually I was told Sushma came from a lower caste. Her parents were very wealthy and they did not want her to be wasted on a poor university lecturer, Brahmin or not. As soon as he had learned of this, he had taken her to live with him.

To me they seemed just as happy, even happier now that they were, presumably, sleeping together. They still retained their own magic and walked through the place as if girded by an invisible and benevolent wall. Where others saw a couple doomed, I saw the irresistible unfolding of a rare love affair. I had never seen such a combination of courtesy, affection, and, I did not doubt it, sexual satisfaction.

Always true to himself, Baschia had made a brilliant move. About fifty miles from the University there was one of India's most famous and ancient Hindu temples. In that place the priests had the power to marry. Before moving in together, Baschia and Sushma had gone to the temple and been married in a ceremony older even than the rituals which attended an arranged marriage. They've managed it, I thought – the perfect combination – a real and free love affair and an ancient, traditional marriage. The idea of this gave me inordinate pleasure. It proved something for both East and West.

The end came very swiftly. I heard it from Dr Mitra who had been part of the drama.

Her parents had arrived. Rich, Dr Mitra explained, Indian merchant rich – professing themselves deeply hurt that their daughter was prepared to ignore her caste and their feelings in this way. It intrigued me that they were opposed to Baschia even though he was from a caste so superior to their own: in English class terms it would represent an advantageous match well worth a businessman's daughter and dowry. Not in India, Dr Mitra insisted: and besides – for he was not without worldliness – they wanted the connection with another wealthy family which a particularly beautiful daughter could bring them.

They had taken over a floor of the best local hotel and, with some difficulty, persuaded the young couple to come and see them. The Head of Police had been there, the Mayor, a most hang-dog Vice-Chancellor of the University, Sushma's two elder brothers who were 'Mafia types' and her three younger sisters who had burst into genuine and affecting tears at the sight of their disgraced sister. Dr Mitra had been there at Baschia's invitation.

The strategy, Dr Mitra explained, grimly, had been to try to separate them. Her father wept and roared; the Head of Police looked solemn and talked about the legality of temple weddings and the danger to public morals of such permissive co-habitation; the Mayor had spoken up for family obedience; the Vice-Chancellor had wrung his hands. Baschia and Sushma had met every objection with serious and sound arguments.

Then her mother had been brought in melodramatically, with cynical manipulation in mind – and Sushma had agreed to go into another room above to talk to her. Baschia's resistance seemed churlish – a mother and her daughter must be allowed to talk privately together. He was overruled. He shook her hand, said Dr Mitra, his eyes misting a little, and gave a little bow. Then he sat down to wait. That was just after 10 p.m.

'We were still in the same room in the same position twelve hours later,' said Dr Mitra, a little shamefacedly. 'Every time Baschia tried to go through to see her, he was blocked by some of the police the Headman had brought along. One by one her family disappeared and we all knew what had happened. They had taken her away. They had kidnapped her.'

Over the next few weeks I saw Baschia every day and every day he seemed more tired, more ill, less and less himself. The message from her parents was that she was free to marry anyone but at the moment was making up her mind. The private information was that she had been locked in her room, was guarded night and day by servants and bodyguards, accompanied even to the bathroom and systematically beaten.

Baschia can do nothing. He has neither the money nor the legal basis to bring an action to retrieve her. He went to their house but was run out of the town by the local police, who are in her parents' pockets. He knows his letters don't reach her. She has been unable to send a single message to him since that last formal handshake.

He knows she will never give in. His feeling for her weakens him daily. There are those, already, who say that he will die quite soon.

2

BOMBAY TAXI
Jamie Rix

The author (the Editor's elder son) fell by the wayside when he and three fellow students won the Perrier Award for Comedy at the Edinburgh Festival in 1982. He became a radio and television producer and director and some of the subsequent awards associated with him are proudly displayed in the foyers of Broadcasting House and the BBC Television Centre: the Sony Award and the Premios Ondes Award for 'Radioactive'; the Sony award for 'In One Ear'; the Montreux Silver Rose for 'KYTV' and a BAFTA Award of 'Smith and Jones'. His other TV productions include 'Faith in the Future', 'Sometime Never', 'Harry Hill's Fruit Fancies', 'How to be a Little Sod' and 'Colin's Sandwich' (which starred Mel Smith and Jamie's sister, Louisa). As a writer he has had six children's books published; the first, Grizzly Tales for Gruesome Kids, *by the percipient Tom Rosenthal, the Publisher of this book, which became the Children's Choice of the Smarties Prize in 1990. This year sees the publication of* The Dreaded Lurgie *(in paperback),* Johnny Casanova – the unstoppable sex machine, Fearsome Tales for Fiendish Kids *and* A Stitch in Time. *In this trip to Bombay, the author and his wife seem to hire a taxi hellbent on acquiring the Indian equivalent of 'the Knowledge'.*

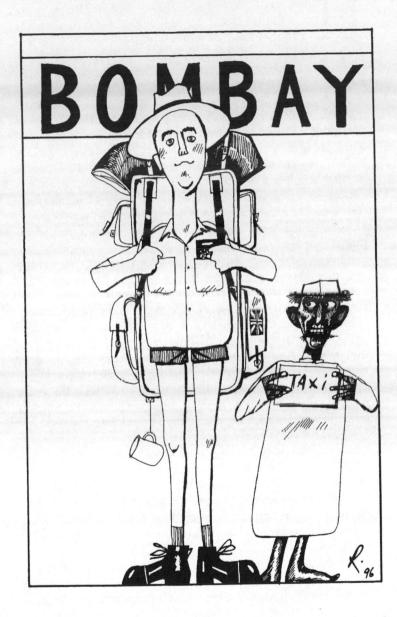

Helen and I arrived at Bombay airport after a marathon flight via the horse-blanket heat of Dubai. We were fresh out of university, soon to be married, and totally unprepared for what was waiting for us on the other side of passport control – a noise that hit us like a swarm of startled starlings, a thumping of plate-glass windows, a sea of desperate faces crying 'Taxi'. It seemed like the whole of Bombay was waiting for us. We were surprised to be so popular. If we hadn't known where we were going we might even have felt intimidated. Luckily Helen's sister, Jacky, had just completed her two-month doctor's elective in southern India. She'd been through this culture shock already. Hers was the voice of experience. 'We'll meet at the Salvation Army Hostel. Get a taxi at the airport,' she'd said, 'and don't let them charge you more than 37 rupees.'

Finding a taxi was the easy bit. We went with the cabbie with the strongest grip. He flung us into the back of his Ambassador like two snatched hostages and skidded away from the kerb before his competitors could overturn his vehicle and have us away. Prior to our kidnap, as we were dragged across the car park, he'd assured us that he knew the precise location of the Salvation Army Hostel and would take us there for the cut-price fare of 50 rupees. We'd beaten him down to 40, and now as we shot along the four-lane highway into the heart of Bombay we were priding ourselves on not looking like nervous, first-time tourists.

In our naïve, Western heads we'd imagined the Salvation Army Hostel to be something akin to a Vauxhall soup kitchen, so it came as something of a surprise when we pulled up outside a marbled tower block that would have satiated the excesses of Ivana Trump. It was the Bombay Hilton and the driver was confused. Didn't all English people stay here? Not us, sadly. We were pound-a-night backpackers.

The driver had started to sweat. His earlier navigational lie was now exposed and we rejoined the highway doing ninety, gently nudging a bicycle rickshaw into the Arabian

Sea. It appeared to be compulsory to drive with one hand glued to the horn and the accelerator flattened to the floor. Suddenly, we were up on two wheels, screeching round a corner into a dusty suburb, where we shuddered to a halt. We were lost again and the driver wound down his window to ask an old man directions. The moment he paused to ponder, a crowd of sixty-plus materialised out of the ether to offer a committee-load of differing opinions. It was about this time that Helen and I started to believe that the Salvation Army Hostel was a cruel figment of Jacky's imagination. But at last, having been pointed to the left, to the right and straight on, our driver reversed out of the neighbourhood and got us firmly back on the wrong road.

Not for long, however. As we bullishly threaded our way past cardboard shanty towns and puddles that doubled as laundrettes, we were leapt upon by a traffic cop. He flung himself across the bonnet and mouthed through the windscreen that our driver should stop, which to our surprise he did. Without so much as a glance at us in the back, the policeman then slid into the passenger seat, pointed franti cally at a vanishing moped and announced melodramatically, 'Follow that Lambretta!' Grateful to be distracted from the search for the elusive Salvation Army Hostel, our driver obeyed and we lurched forward into a scene from *Bullitt*, hurtling through the Bombay backstreets like Steve McQueen, overturning small women and children and frightening the chili vendors. Helen and I were pressed against the back seat like wet clay in a wind tunnel. Our hot skin had stuck to the plastic cover and our thighs were flayed to the bone.

After about half an hour, and with the petrol gauge flashing empty, the driver deliberately lost the scooter down a narrow alleyway. The traffic cop yawned, pushed his cap up off his eyes, tapped the dashboard twice, brought the taxi to an emergency halt and turned to face us.

'Thank you,' he said politely, getting out to see where he was. Before he could disappear, I seized the opportunity to pick his brains.

'Do you know where the Salvation Army Hostel is?' I asked. He indicated to the left, to the right and straight on. It was just behind us. And the driver charged us 135 rupees for the detour.

Being nervous, first-time tourists, we paid.

3

DO YOU COME HERE OFTEN?
Jonathan Rix

The author (the Editor's younger son) also crossed the Rubicon when he won the Best New Playwright Award at the Stephen Joseph Festival in 1983. He is now a writer of plays and novels, the teacher of loud children and, until recently, the Arts Council/ Home Office writer-in-residence at H.M.P. Gartree. The residency was on a daily basis, just to keep the record straight! He, too, had his first Betty Trask award-winning novel, Some Hope, published by the perspicacious Tom Rosenthal of André Deutsch and has also won a Gulbenkian Award and a Galleries Award for Basic English Tour Guides of historic sites. In this little tale he covers many countries of the world and its peoples, ending, appropriately enough for Part IV of this book, in Sri Lanka.

A prime factor in any trip that we take is the people that we meet on the way.

There was the fresh-from-America 22-year-old I met on a beach in Egypt who informed me that she could not bear the filth and stench of that country any longer and was therefore going to get the hell out and go to spick-and-span India instead.

There was the coach driver I met in Aswan who invited me back to his house for a bite to eat, and then proceeded

to take all his clothes off and with the subtlety of a dead donkey ask whether the English had hair 'down there'.

There was a Frenchman who set his Alsatian on me because the *Anglais* had sunk their fleet during the Second World War.

There was the Belgian couple in Nepal, one of whom was so loud and so rude that his friend had to walk behind him handing out gifts to any of the locals he had insulted so that the two of them would not be lynched.

There was the man I had to share a tent with in Iceland during a thirty-six-hour rainstorm, who smelt so bad that every time he rolled over a waft of the vilest stench would drift from his sleeping bag so that I spent the whole day and a half caught in a battle with my rising bile, teeth clenched to stop me throwing up and making matters even worse.

There was the woman I met when I was an innocent 17-year-old on the streets of New York at three in the morning who informed me when I asked her the time that it was 'twenty-five dollars'.

There was the Dutch woman who suddenly lifted up her skirt, dropped it over the head of a very drunk friend of mine with the words 'Come into my tent', and then told any of us who could hear, 'I think it's time for the boat to enter the harbour.'

There was the man who broke both legs falling off the roof of a hotel in Corfu – where I was a holiday rep – after he had tried to swing onto his mates' balcony so he could go 'boo', and who then tried to sue the company because he hadn't been able to finish his holiday.

There was the Albanian with whom I spent a morning drinking some viciously powerful home-made raki, who within the space of an hour had a blazing row with our interpreter, gushed with romantic joy about the virtues of his country, giggled and giggled at jokes only he understood, and finally stood sobbing when it came to the time of our departure as if at the funeral of a deeply beloved grandmother.

There was the Greek chief of police who spent forty-five

minutes trying to convince me I was not a proper man because I was wearing an earring.

There was the café owner in Tirana who approached us and asked, 'Do you speak English?' and when we said, 'Yes', smiled politely and told us: 'Good. We are closed.'

There was the 40-year-old black Johannesburg doorman who informed a 13-year-old me that he had to call me 'Sir' or 'Master Jonathan' and not Jonty because otherwise he would lose his job.

There was the Greek pizza bar owner who shot the owner of the pizza bar next door, and when a year later he was released from prison went into business with the victim, who had just got out of hospital. And jolly good pizzas they made.

There was the Nepali Customs Officer who asked us if we were carrying any drugs and when we told him 'No', said 'That's okay, you can buy plenty here.'

But my favourite travelling encounter was with a man my wife and I met in Sri Lanka. He informed us he was an airline pilot, owned a tea plantation, was a devout Buddhist and that his wife was a former Miss Sri Lanka. We went to Kandy with this man, convinced he was a con artist but delighted by the height of his tales and the warmth of his company. Sure enough he spent two days trying to con us out of money, taking us around in a taxi driven by someone he claimed was his valet. Rugs, gemstones, art work . . . he tried to get us to buy everything. Finally, having made about ten pounds out of us (not bad for two days' work in Sri Lanka) he decided he'd had enough and so had we. We both made our excuses, both parties claiming that we were heading out of town that evening. Next morning arrived and we were having breakfast and who should appear at the door, rotate and disappear as fast as he had come? Why, if it wasn't our friendly Buddhist guide come to get his commission from our hotel owner – the commission we had already told the owner we wanted deducted from our bill. We could not leave him this way. So we wrote him the following note.

Dear—,
Thank you so much for all your kindness and consideration over the past few days. We are so sorry that we never got to meet your family or to see your lovely home.

We just hope that in another life we will have a chance to meet again and that when we do you will be our tourist and we will be your guide.

All our love and thanks.
Jonty and Caroline.

Don't people make it all so worthwhile?

4

WHAT'S IN A NAME?
Brian Rix

For his third, and last, appearance in this book, the author/editor visits Portugal and causes confusion with his old-fashioned passport and his new-fangled driving licence. He was indeed lucky to get out of the country with so little trouble to return to his native heath. Unlike Lemuel Gulliver, on reaching England's shores from the Iberian peninsula he did not find anyone or anything particularly odious – other than the pushing and shoving at the luggage carousel in Heathrow's Terminal 1, that is.

There's an old joke about a bloke who enters a monastery, takes a vow of silence, but every fifth year is allowed a brief chat with the abbot. The first five years go by and our friend the monk, no longer a novice, is granted his opening interview. 'Well, my son,' says the abbot, 'what concerns you?' 'The food's pretty monotonous,' comes the reply. Five more years pass. 'At this second discourse, have you any further concerns?' queries the abbot. 'My bed's rather hard,' says the monk. Another five years move on. Once more the monk stands in front of his superior. 'I fear, father, that I must renounce this monastic life and return to the wider world outside.' 'Thank God for that,' responds the abbot. 'You've done nothing but bloody grumble since you got here.'

211

I feel rather like that monk. My third story for *Gullible's Travails* and once more I am whingeing about foreign travel – or rather some part of it. I am not a Europhobe; simply that, of late, I seem to have run into a spot of bother when venturing from these shores, particularly when trying to explain matters to my fellow Europeans who do not have, shall we say, a command of the English language – for I certainly do not have a command of their particular mother tongues. The first sign of trouble was last April on that abortive trip to Paris, whilst the second was August in Portugal. There we were in our hired hillside villa, entirely surrounded by burnt-out eucalyptus trees – the wind changed and we were rapidly transformed into something resembling refugees from the old Black and White Minstrel Show. Yet another aborted overseas mission and an early return to good old Blighty. For once, though, I approached passport control at the airport with a certain degree of trepidation. Let me explain . . .

Two nights before our early exeunt from the Iberian peninsula, we were enjoying dinner at a local caff a couple of kilometres down the hill. Tucking into our chicken piri-piri and chips, omelette and chips, presunto and chips, swordfish and chips, tomato salad and chips and chips with chips, we suddenly heard the very loud hooting of a horn from a battered car careering down the hill. The honking continued for some minutes as the jalopy ground to a halt by the entrance to our terrace and within moments loud Portuguese shouting and swearing came from several sweating locals, joined – eventually – by a screaming lady who seemed to have been working in the kitchen and obviously had a chip on her shoulder or other fish to fry. After some time the noise subsided and we were left in rather nervous peace. Actually 'left' is the correct word, for the staff – who seemed to be embroiled in some industrial dispute – had upped and gone and only one very courteous, but very slow, old man was left to totter around with our plates. Having waited some forty minutes for our ice-creams and coffees we, too, decided to abandon ship, return

WHAT'S IN A NAME?

to our somewhat sooty villa and rummage through the fridge there for our desserts.

Paying the bill wasn't too easy, either. The signs on the door displayed the proud fact that the café accepted Visa, Access, Diners, Barclaycard, MasterCard, Eurocard, American Express – the lot. In fact, the machine accepted none of them – it had been out-of-order all day, it seemed, or even longer – and we were left scratting around searching our pockets and wallets for the necessary escudos and centimos to settle matters.

Settle! I was the first to leave and – being the eldest, white-haired patriarch of the party – was immediately confronted by a puce, perspiring Portuguese, who turned out to be the proprietor.

'Please,' he said, 'please, you are English, no?' I agreed that I was. 'I am most sorry,' he went on, 'but did you hear a klaxon toot during your dinner?' I hasten to add that my written translation of his English is clearer in print than in person. Anyway, I once more agreed that I had indeed heard a klaxon toot. 'I am so sorry,' he went on, 'but did you hear it klaxonning down two times?' Two times! We'd heard it klaxonning down about ten times. I said so. By now the proprietor was wreathed in smiles, garlic, vinho verde and gratitude. 'Will you tell the policia, please? I am so sorry to disturb you. I am the owner of this hotel and restaurant (sic). His klaxonning and his tooting worries you all.'

I was about to agree that this would be a normal reaction when I suddenly realised that there, standing in the gloaming, were two local guardians of the law, heavily armed and totally bemused, questioning the original, klaxonning miscreant who, for good measure, was shouting furious imprecations and accusations in the general direction of my newly found friend who, in turn, obviously thought some further explanation was necessary:

'He is drunk. He came klaxonning down two times. It is not allowed all over the world to klaxon and toot at night. I come out and tell him he is disturbing my guests. He

klaxons and toots again. My staff, they leave. I telephone
the policia. I tell them to bring their balloon. He is drunk. I
have been to England twelve times and they would bring
their balloon if you ask them, no?'

I agreed they probably would bring their balloon but,
judging by the fumes assailing me, I thought they would
probably use their balloon on both parties concerned. I
thought that, mind you. I felt it was hardly politic to go into
details.

'Please,' said my perspiring Portuguese prop., 'please tell
them you hear the klaxon tooting two times and give them
your name. I am so sorry to disturb you.'

I weakly protested that I was only there on holiday, and
by now my wife and entire family were nodding vigorously
but negatively, terrified (as I was) that if I gave my name
and local address it wouldn't be too long before something
more akin to a police siren than a klaxon would be tooting
around our persons and property.

'Please,' pleaded the proprietor. 'You see he is telling
them I kick his car. I did so. I lose my brains. It is not good
to lose the brains, I know. Is bad and I kick his car.' It was
so battered, one little extra dent would scarcely have made
any difference – but it did change the scenario. The klaxonning drunk was obviously counter-claiming for damage to
his property. I tried to leave – but then a young guarda
approached and asked to see my passport. I knew then I
was in for a long evening . . .

The little window in my passport has written in full 'The
Right Honourable Lord Rix CBE' whilst, inside, it goes a
little further – 'The Right Honourable Brian Norman Roger
Lord Rix Kt CBE'. In the flickering light from the barbecue
and the fags which were being chain-smoked by the local
law, attempts were made to decipher who I was. 'RIX,' I
shouted, 'those other words and letters are titles.'

My proprietor pal was overwhelmed. After all, he had
been to England twelve times. He knew a toff when he saw
one. The local fuzz, on the other hand, were totally
unmoved. 'Dom' would have done a damn sight better.

'You are a lord,' genuflected the prop. 'In Parliament?' That was the second time that had been said to me that year. Once, on a marooned Eurostar, by a French guard – now in Portugal, at a roadside caff. But it gave me a great idea for my address. When the guarda asked me for that I bellowed 'Houses of Parliament, London' with great conviction – but even he, who could only speak about four words of English (four more than I can speak of Portuguese), was not fooled.

'Driving licence,' was his reply.

This, displaying my Christian names following 'Lord Rix CBE DL', added to the confusion about my exact nomenclature – but he could now see my Wimbledon address. Then: '*Here*, where?' It was my turn to be obtuse. 'In the cars, everyone' – and half the family moved off in one, whilst mine filled up with the balance, except for me. Taking a deep breath, I bellowed: 'Heard the klaxon. Won't appear as witness. Write to me' – leapt into my car and drove off.

No one followed. No blue lights and sirens trailed up the hill. The next day, as we evacuated our sooty villa and returned to Heathrow via Faro, nobody even bothered to look at my passport at either airport, anyway. But I suppose I could still receive an official letter, demanding my presence back in Portugal as a vital witness in the case of a klaxonning drunk *v* a proprietor who lost his brains. I think I shall pretend it never arrived. I have only been in Portugal two times – but I haven't, as yet, lost *my* brains.

And who will I be, anyway? Mr Wright, Miss Honora Bell, Mr Lord, Mr Knight, Mr C. Bee or Mr Dyell.

I might even be Mr Brian, Mr Norman or Mr Roger. But you can be absolutely certain I won't be Lord Rix.

Frankly, my dear, I don't give a toot.

ENVOI

In truth, this is the final word. I am not a little pleased that this compilation can possibly meet with no censurers: for what objections can be made against writers who relate only plain fact or fiction, where they have not the least interest with respect either to trade or negotiations? They have written for the noblest end: to inform, instruct or amuse mankind and without any view towards profit or praise. I never suffered a word to pass that could possibly give the least offence even to those who are most ready to take it. So I hope I may with justice pronounce myself an editor, compiler and author perfectly blameless, against whom the tribe of answerers, considerers, observers, reflecters, detecters, remarkers, will never be able to find matter for exercising their talents.

But this description of a detestable tribe doth by no means affect the British nation, who may be an example to the whole world for their wisdom, care and justice when it comes to supporting worthy causes including, by the purchase of this book of travails, Mencap's Blue Sky Appeal.

I here take a final leave of my courteous readers and return to enjoy the sound of our Appeals Department counting the spondulicks; I also entreat those who have any tincture of covetousness to place this on one side and respond with generosity and warmth of heart to my pleas; otherwise, I must command that they will not presume to appear in my sight.

The Editor